Tales of
KOEHLER HOLLOW

Books by Christopher A. Brooks

I Never Walked Alone: The Autobiography of an American Singer
(with Shirley Verrett)

*Follow Your Heart: Moving with the Giants of Jazz, Swing and
Rhythm and Blues* (with Joe Evans)

Dangerous Intimacy: Ten African American Men Living with HIV
(with Christopher Coleman)

African American Almanac (general editor)

Through the Voices of Men: South African Men Speak about HIV
(First and Second Edition)

Roland Hayes: The Legacy of an American Tenor
(with Robert Sims)

The Most Vulnerable: Women, HIV and Islam in Mali

*Dual Pandemics: HIV and the Coronavirus
in Several Kenyan Communities*

Tales of
KOEHLER HOLLOW

An African American Family in Rural Appalachia

by

Naomi Hodge-Muse

Christopher A. Brooks

UNSUNG
VOICES
BOOKS

Typesetting and ebook creation provided by

L4C Design Services, Inc.

A Living 4 Creativity Company

living4creativity.com

ISBN 978-1-964495-00-2

Printed in the United States of America

unsungvoicesbooks.com

8   7   6   5   4

This work is dedicated to the memory
of
Thomas J. Brown

Tales of Koehler Hollow
Table of Contents

Preface
Shaking the Tree

*S*ituated at the top of a steep hill in mountainous Fieldale, Virginia, is a wooded acre known as Mountain Top Cemetery. This now-abandoned land was deeded by a White benefactor, John Rangeley, to the trustees of the once-adjacent Mountain Top African Methodist Episcopal Colored Church in the mid-1870s. Fewer than one hundred souls are buried at Mountain Top Cemetery. There are several professionally carved and engraved markers, but most sites are identified by a single brick-sized stone. Other graves are marked by nothing more than a slight indentation in the ground.

The Mountain Top AME Church has long since disappeared. The last known burial in the cemetery took place in 1968.

From the time I first visited Mountain Top Cemetery in August 2016, I sensed this place would be significant. I saw grave markers for James Alfred Finney (1930–1967), Howard McGhee

(d. 1940), Joe Waller (1869–1921), and little Annette Evone Riley (1953–1957). I learned that among the unmarked graves were the remains of George Washington Finney (1880–1964) and his wife, Rosa Belle Waller Finney (1883–1968), who was reportedly the last to be buried at Mountain Top. Also laid to rest there are George and Rosa's daughter, Anna B. Finney (1908–1936), and their great-granddaughter, Loretta Maria Hodge (1952–1964). However, it was not until I stood at the grave of the once-enslaved family matriarch, Amy Finney (1850–1936), the source of this family legacy and whose property is at the center of this book, that things began to crystallize in my mind.

On that desolate, yet sacred, ground in modern day Henry County, Virginia, I realized that for the second time in my professional career, I would be responsible for bringing to life the story of a formerly enslaved Black woman. It was also then that I understood how this work would transcend what was originally to have been a series of loosely connected historical family vignettes surrounding a homestead known as Koehler Hollow (pronounced as "holla").

Only gradually did I comprehend the gravity and the enormity of this project and frankly I was intimidated by what lay ahead as I left Martinsville very early the following morning. I had no question about my ability to tell the story, but I didn't see a clear strategy for doing so. Telling the story of the descendants of this formerly enslaved woman was different from my book on Roland Hayes,[1] where I had many papers and preserved documents to consult. I easily constructed a chronology and could proceed with writing the book. Additionally, Hayes left a 1942 autobiographical account. Even though it contained several intentional omissions and other shortcomings, it provided an overview of his life up to the early 1940s.

Naomi Hodge-Muse is Koehler Hollow's principal advocate. She was absolutely determined that her family's story be told. Her many hours spent on Ancestry.com and laboring in local libraries and the Henry County Courthouse researching the tiniest details, also made my job smoother. Capturing Naomi's authorial voice took some time. As I mastered her speech patterns, vocabulary, and regional terminology, a clearer path to writing this work gradually emerged. She and I interviewed more than twenty people either individually or jointly, which required numerous trips to Henry County from the Richmond area. In that part of the Commonwealth, there was still some hesitancy in speaking to an "outsider," even though I am also an African American. One of the more challenging tasks was getting those who lived through the Martinsville Seven case (Chapter 9) in the late 1940s to speak about their recollections of that gross miscarriage of justice. A few went on record, but often in hushed tones and with the criterion that their names not be used in the telling of that sad story, even more than sev-

---

[1] Brooks and Sims, *Roland Hayes: The Legacy of an American Tenor* (Indiana University Press, 2015).

enty years after those young men were executed for the crime of rape. Casting that narrative in the context of Naomi's Uncle Sunny Boy, who was not only a contemporary but who knew several of those accused young men, was an added layer to this story. Only after Sunny Boy was drafted into the US Army and out of the region did Naomi's great-grandfather feel that his precious Sunny Boy was safe from any reprisals in the aftermath of that court case. Only the recently late Miss Alberta Wilson (who passed away in March 2024 at 101) felt comfortable discussing the incident without any restrictions.

Transforming more than fifty vignettes into the present form was also challenging and was the most rigorous part of constructing this book. In the end, however, Naomi and I are pleased with the results and firmly believe that this is an important story about an underexplored American experience that needs to be told.

Unlike Roland Hayes, no one in this family has become internationally renowned, sung on the Metropolitan Opera stage,[2] or won a major award for their accomplishments. This story, however, describes the rich lived experience of African Americans in Appalachia from the mid-19th century to the present, complete with the accompanying complications, joys, tragedies, and sorrows.

---

[2] Verrett and Brooks, *I Never Walked Alone: The Autobiography of an American Singer* (John Wiley, 2003).

I met Naomi Hodge-Muse in late 2012. She is president of several area organizations, including Martinsville's chapter of the NAACP and the Voter's League. She served as president of the local Sierra Club and is also an Elder in Presbyterian Church USA. In her leadership capacity within those organizations, she has put her name and reputation on the line for numerous causes, including a successful effort to block uranium mining in the region. When she and I began discussing her activist record in southwestern Virginia, she said that it came to her because her great-grandfather, George Washington Finney, who raised her, had also been a community leader in his time, as had her late husband, William B. Muse, Jr.

More fundamentally, Naomi Hodge-Muse has made many personal sacrifices and neglected her personal life in the interest of protecting and advancing the aims of her family. She delayed marriage until she was well into her thirties. She did not have children who could inherit from her directly. This work has become her testament of what she wants the world to know about her, her family, and her local community surroundings.

These narratives are a microcosm of larger regional and national society. Whether for the formerly enslaved Amy, her children, or their descendants, much of their lives were lived within the confines of a system that devalued them and their humanity. Most were unwilling to accept second-class citizenship. Sometimes that family grit and defiance served them well; on other occasions, less so. They certainly were not the stereotypical broken and bowing people often portrayed in popular media. Yet, the African American Appalachian experience was different from those living in more urban areas.

This family's 150-year journey reflects the racial codes that defined much of that time. It is a part of Americana that is seldom written about and "not spoken of." As one of my informants plainly stated, "That's a tree you don't want to shake."

Christopher A. Brooks
Professor of Anthropology
Virginia Commonwealth University

1

Koehler Hollow: A House on a Hill

I always thought the world stopped at that mailbox at the bottom of the hill. Our official address was Route 3 (later renamed Harmon Hill Road), Box 465. The mile-long walk up that unpaved road leading to the big house seemed like traveling through another world. As you walked up that red dirt road of the Hollow, on the left the hillside was lined with mountain laurels in the spring. The aroma of those plants was unmistakable. The surrounding mountains were also full of gooseberries, blackberries, blueberries, and raspberries. We learned at a young age that all those berries were edible and collected them for pies and other desserts. But those mountain laurels, beautiful as they are, are poisonous to humans.

As you continued up the Hollow, you passed by the Lawsons' on the left. They were a White family who refused to chain their aggressive German Shepherd. That dog was awful.

My Aunt Wootsie even used a stick with nails in it to keep that animal at bay. My younger brother routinely came running home terrified because that beast had chased him. One day I had enough. I got one of Poppa's old machetes and went down the road and stood out in front of the Lawsons' house and shouted at that dog with my machete poised, "Come on out here! Come on! Come bite somebody not scared of you, 'cause I'm a cut you right here so everybody can see it."

You can't tell me that dogs don't have good sense because that dog realized that crazy girl standing there with her machete was ready to send him to dog heaven or hell. He just looked at me, not moving a muscle. He didn't even bark. It wasn't a week before the Lawsons had put a fence around that yard, and that dog no longer chased anyone else.

Continuing up that hill about a quarter mile on the left was the remains of Great-Grandma Amy's house. It was a relatively simple but sturdy cottage that had been built in the 1890s after she purchased the land. It had a kitchen and a bedroom that doubled as a living room. The kitchen had a stove that kept the place warm. After my parents, Doretha (pronounced DOE - Ree - THA) and Jesse Ben Hodge, married in the late 1940s, they lived in Grandma Amy's house, but it burned down in the early 1950s. I'll come to that story later. About fifteen hundred feet from where Great-Grandma Amy's house stood the house that my grandmother, Grandma Dollie, built. I believe she built it in the late 1930s and that's where she raised her daughter and son, Doretha and Uncle Sunny Boy.

At various times, Grandma Dollie moved into the main house and Poppa rented her place.

About another thousand feet up a small hill facing the door of Grandma Dollie's house was the main homestead, Koehler Hollow. Poppa, George Washington Finney, built this house in 1924. This is the only dwelling that still stands today and is the basis for most of what I have to say. My sisters and brother were all born in that main house and that's where our family values were formed. Many of the lessons that we learned were taught to us in that very dwelling.

We kept multiple gardens at Koehler Hollow. There was one beside the house and one below the house. There was a chicken coop above the house and a pigpen a little further out. We were totally self-sufficient on that land. We had a huge black pot in which we made lye soap and heated water for washing the clothes outside. There was a spring under the road with a massive oak tree nearby. It took my brother David, my sisters Loretta and Christine, and me circling hand to hand to surround that huge tree.

The big house itself was white with a long porch. Poppa built a trellis and planted silver lace vine right across the top of the porch, which provided ample shade, even in the midst of summer. We nicknamed the hill in front of our house "Rattlesnake Mountain" because that's where Doretha and Aunt Wootsie killed what seemed to be a huge rattlesnake. We essentially lived in a valley because there were mountains in every direction as far as the eye could see.

Even in his seventies, my great-grandfather took us walking through the woods and taught us how to track all kinds of animals. He also taught us how to live in peace with nature and preached that we should only take from it what we needed. Poppa said you didn't kill anything unless it was for survival purposes. We couldn't even put a bug in a jar and let it die. We could put one in and study it, but after fifteen minutes we had to let it go. Poppa didn't let us kill a lizard or a snake because, according to him, it had a right to live. He pointed out an area and said, "That's a rabbit path. See that tunnel of bushes, that's what he will slide through if he's being chased." An untrained eye wouldn't have noticed it, but Poppa showed us how to spot it.

He took us on these excursions two to three times a month. Poppa also taught us how to identify deer tracks and how to tell when people walked through the woods. He showed us how twigs and leaves get turned and branches bend, marking human and animal movement.

The winters at Koehler Hollow could be excruciatingly cold. The hoar frost first showed up in November. Those little tiny ice crystals that popped out of the moist ground would be the first indicator of how severe a winter we would face. In December, the snow began. It snowed from then until March sometimes. Some weeks it snowed every other day. I remember one year, when I was about ten, it snowed every Wednesday for a month. It got so deep at points we couldn't get under the house to the root cellar.

Our family canned all summer long in preparation for the winter. We canned beans, tomatoes, peas, preserves, and other produce. But this particular winter we hadn't brought enough out of the cellar for an extended snow. The snow had blocked the root cellar entrance completely shut. We got down to our last cans of vegetables. Grandma Dollie made a big pot of soup using the ingredients she pieced together. She and Doretha made the kids sit down and eat. The others gulped down their soup, but I didn't want to eat mine, because I knew Grandma Dollie and Doretha were hungry. Doretha was always hungry. They also made sure that Momma Rosie and Poppa ate, although Poppa protested as well. Finally, Doretha told me, "You sit there and eat that soup, gal. I mean it." I did so, but it was full of tears. I think that was the closest we ever came to starving. Luckily, the sun came within a day or so and melted the snow enough for us to get under the house to the root cellar. To be sure, Doretha had many flaws, but her motherly instincts were well intact that winter when she placed our needs above her own.

My family's direct ancestral line dates to the mid-nineteenth century to Amy Finney, my-great-great grandmother. Grandma Amy was born on an unknown date in 1850 and enslaved on the Mitchell Plantation in present day Henry County, Virginia. Although she was a "Mitchell" for at least the first fifteen years of her life, after the Civil War some of those who had been enslaved chose not to keep their enslavers' surname. Amy grew to hate the Mitchell name, so she adopted "Finney," the surname of her father's people. While several of her brothers and sisters kept the Mitchell surname, Amy wanted nothing to do with it. Even today, we have blood relatives who are Mitchells and those who are Finneys.

Amy's father had come from the Finney Plantation in Franklin County and had been an accomplished carpenter. It was common for such skilled enslaved persons to be hired out to another plantation and that's what happened to Amy's father. The carpentry profession remained in our family line for the next several generations. At least two of Amy's sons became skilled carpenters. Her youngest son, George, or "Poppa" as we called him, became a master carpenter.

Amy's parents had to have been big people, because she was a solidly built woman who stood about six feet tall, with big arms, legs, and feet. She never learned to read or write, but that didn't stop her from negotiating fees for the services she provided as a midwife, plowing fields, cooking, or doing other manual jobs.

During the Reconstruction Era, formerly enslaved men and women were offered the right to buy land on the very plantations on which they had once been held in bondage. In 1890, an emancipated and hard-working Amy purchased an acre of land a little more than a mile from the house in which she had once worked as a servant. She built a small cottage on the land and raised her family. She also built a barn, where she maintained her animals, especially her prized workhorses, which she kept in pristine shape. Some thirty years later, George purchased several acres adjacent to his mother's original land.

It's very important to understand that Grandma Amy Finney was not raised in kindness. The horrors she experienced during her childhood enslavement made her a hard and, at times, a mean woman. Those qualities were no doubt fostered in her early years and apparently never left her. Some of her children and grandchildren witnessed her severe character firsthand and remembered it quite clearly.

Whenever I pass a tobacco field in this area, I remember a story that Poppa told me. His mother had passed it on to him when our people were enslaved in Henry County. When enslaved children were about four or five, they were taken to the tobacco fields and made to remove horn worms from the tobacco stems. If a child was skittish or afraid about pulling the worms, the overseer would come and put one of the green worms in the child's mouth and hold it shut until the child swallowed it. This was to cure the child of any squeamishness. Is there any reason to doubt that Amy became such a tough woman?

Amy married a man named Peter Finney, so her surname remained Finney after she married. He was probably a cousin of some sort. We don't know much about Amy's first husband, but four children were born as a result: Susan A. Finney (1871–1936); Ben Finney (1873–?, named after her younger brother); King Finney (1877–1940), and George Washington Finney (1880–1964). We believe her second child, Ben, was not the birth child of Peter Finney because of his light complexion. Those kinds of "relationships" were not all that unusual in this part of the world. Without question, however, George was Amy's favorite and most devoted child.

* * * * * * * * * * *

People came around from all over to get their annual spring tonic from Momma Rosie. As a seventy-three-year-old woman who was raised in southwest Virginia, I grew up on an annual spring tonic treatment. Momma Rosie, Grandma Dollie, and Doretha conferred on what ingredients they needed from the woods.

I can remember them using root vein, sassafras, and the very first sprouts of a pine tree. There were other ingredients, but those are the ones I remember. These were boiled all day. It smelled pretty good when they put the sassafras in, but once the pine sprout was put in, it changed the whole flavor of things. The smell grew pretty rough. After this concoction boiled all day, they would set it out and let it cool. The women then added a little bootleg to it. The following morning, we all got tonic. It tasted pretty bad; I thought it tasted like Griffin shoe polish. It sure smelled like it. We had to open our mouths and take a whole tablespoon of this glop.

Within hours of taking the tonic, little fine rashes broke out all over our bodies. When Momma Rosie saw the rashes, which sometimes itched, she'd say, "It's workin'. Now It's runnin' the poison out yo' body." We also got "wormed" once a year. Kids in the area used to get these pinworms in their systems and grown folks gave us worm medicine. Pinworms would enter your system through all manner of ways, like bedsheets, or casual contact with someone carrying them. Young children were the most susceptible to pinworm infections.

Believe it or not, the pinworm treatment was a teaspoon of turpentine oil and sugar. It didn't matter if you didn't want to take it. If you resisted, some grown-up would grab you, hold your nostrils together, and wrap their legs around your body so you couldn't kick or run. They'd open your mouth and down it went. Then, sure enough, the worms came out in your stool. Momma Rosie or Grandma Dollie often inspected our elimination to see if there were any live pinworms in what we had expelled.

We also wore an acifidity bag. That is a folk remedy that most people have no clue of unless they are from southern Appalachia. It was a foul-smelling paste that you got from the pharmacy, unless you had a homemade one. It was put in a little piece of fabric which was tied tight around the neck with a little string. It was supposed to ward off colds and the flu, but some of the old people believed that they protected us from evil spirits as well.

It seemed that everybody wore them. When you became a teenager, you didn't have to wear the little dirty string around your neck. Your acifidity bag was pinned to your underskirt.

Doretha tried a home remedy on Christine when she got the mumps. She made a poultice with onions and mustard and some other ingredients. She put this paste in a cloth and wrapped it around Christine's neck. The next morning when we woke up, Christine was crying in pain. When Doretha removed the poultice from around her neck, it had taken off the entire top layer of her skin. My sister is chocolate brown, but there was a pink ring around her neck. The poultice was too strong. Doretha became frightened and took her to our family doctor in Martinsville. Dr. Williams was shocked to see Chrissy's neck. He told Doretha if she didn't stop practicing medicine, he was going to have her thrown in jail. Some of those home remedies worked and others, like in the case of Christine, didn't.

But that didn't make Doretha stop practicing folk remedies. I was a severe asthmatic and she took me up to Covington, an hour's drive each way, to a roots man who was said to have a remedy for asthma. Of course, it was nothing more than another tonic which tasted worse than the others I had already been exposed to. It didn't cure my asthma.

Mountain people also had a remedy for fever that was called "tansy." It was made from a yellow flower. They used it to cure several illnesses like parasites and worm infestations (especially in children). It could also be used for someone suffering from a severe headache and could stimulate someone's appetite after an illness. Garlic was used typically as a remedy for high blood pressure. The person affected would just chew it all day.

There was an internal liniment for menstrual cramps that a man who peddled Rawleigh products sold. That company marketed all kinds of remedies including lotions, medicinal salves, and ointments. Their menstrual cramp treatment required a teaspoon of the product in some hot water with sugar. I know that remedy worked for me. It must have contained a muscle relaxer because it would put me right to sleep and when I woke up the cramps were gone. That same man from Rawleigh drove his car throughout Henry County. In the trunk of his car he had all kinds of things from bucket menders to repair buckets which had sprung a leak to medicines for animals.

Momma Rosie made lye soap every year. It was made of renderings (leftover fat from hogs after slaughter), ashes, and store-bought Red Devil Lye. Momma Rosie had a huge pot in front of the house where she boiled the hog lard, ashes, and lye the entire day. The kids had to go to the woods and bring more wood to keep the fire hot. The smell of the lye soap was horrendous.

By the end of the day, Momma Rosie would call the chickens around with cornbread. Once she got hold of a chicken, she'd pull out a tail feather. She'd put the single feather in the lye soap. If the tail feather came out without any feathers on the stem, the soap was ready. After the liquid cooled a little, men came along and poured it into a tin about eight deep and six feet long. That's where the soap mixture caked and hardened. It could then be broken off into squares for use. It had a kind of *Beverly Hillbillies* feel to it, but we made it work. It was like using 1930s technology in the 1950s and 60s.

We had some good times at the Hollow. When we were young, David and I terrorized one chick that grew into a huge, majestic Dominicker rooster with black and white speckles. As beautiful as he was, he also grew up to be mean and ornery.

What's more, after he was grown, that rooster carried a grudge and did not like me or David. When we came home from school, we'd have to run fast to make it on the porch after we passed the hedge in the yard, because that rooster would lie in wait behind the hedge and pounce on us. Once he even flew up and attacked from the air. We were shocked that huge creature could become airborne.

One afternoon, the rooster had gotten the best of us. He had scratched David and me, so we were especially agitated. Christine had left her doll on the back porch and despite the fact that the rooster was lurking outside, she was determined to get it. We told her not to because that rooster was in a particularly bad mood that day. Of course, "Miss Perfect" didn't listen. She went out to get her doll and sure enough that rooster flew up and scratched her in the face. Christine screamed. At about the same time, Aunt Wootsie had come in the house and was sitting down having her weekly cup of bootleg after a week of working as a domestic. We ran down the steps and told Wootsie what had happened. She took one look at Christine, who was still sobbing from the rooster attack and said, "I've had enough of that damn rooster." She got up and said, "Y'all go and fetch me that foot tub." Well, we knew what that meant. That rooster's time among the living was waning. Wootsie went out and threw down some cornbread and called out, "Here chickey, chickey, chickey." She just sat and waited for that devil bird to show up. The chickens started coming around and that huge Dominicker rooster came strutting as if he owned the place. The other chickens even made way for him. Without so much as a blink, Wootsie grabbed that rooster by the legs and held it. When the rooster began flapping its wings, he looked even larger than we realized. He attempted to swing his body around to peck Wootsie into turning him loose, but she kept her arm out of its way. That demon bird put up a brave fight. I believe he even drew a little blood from his assailant. But in the end, Wootsie was too much for him. It seemed like she had an ironclad grip on him. "Where's that foot tub, chillun?" she called out. We kept our distance while she fought that rooster, because had it escaped we knew he would come straight for us for having told Wootsie about him. I found the foot tub, moved it over to her, and cleared right out. Wootsie took that tub, put it upside down, and threw that devil bird under so only his head was sticking out. He was squawking away at that point. Wootsie told David, "Come stand on this tub, boy!" When Christine and I realized the bird was subdued, we came and stood on the foot tub with him. Wootsie took that hatchet and with one clean chop took that rooster's head clear off. His body continued flapping under the tub. After a while, there was no movement. It was a glorious day!

Wootsie went in the house and started boiling some water and then came back outside and started plucking the feathers off that bird. She then cut off the rooster's toes. When those toes came off, I thought to myself, "Those toes would make a great necklace." I told Christine to fetch me some thread.

She and I were going to have matching chicken-toe necklaces. Once I finished sewing the necklaces, Christine and I put them around our necks. David wasn't interested in a necklace, but we all took off our shirts, went to the foot tub where the rooster's blood was, dipped our fingers in the blood and made ourselves some war paint. After decorating our faces with the blood, we started dancing around like Indians singing, "Hey yah, yah, yah, hey yah, yah, yah." We celebrated our victory over that wicked rooster who was dead at last.

Just as we were dancing, up the hill came a Yellow cab. That was unusual because we didn't ride Yellow cabs, we always rode in the black cabs. We stopped a moment and looked. It was Doretha with groceries. The White cab driver got out of the car and took one look at these little Black children with no shirts on, hair in total disarray, blood all on our faces, and chicken-toe necklaces. Doretha was so embarrassed she told the driver to place the groceries at the door of the car and not worry about helping her bring them in the house. That cab driver lit out of the Hollow and left a cloud of dust as he drove off. He must have surely thought we were practicing some kind of voodoo ritual.

Doretha went into the house where Wootsie was still tending to that rooster. "Wootsie, you damn fool! You got my chaps out here acting like 'heatherons'." "What?" Wootsie said. "What'd you mean lettin' these kids dance around that foot tub with blood on their faces? You make me sick." Aunt Wootsie didn't know we had been outside dancing with chicken blood war paint.

Every one of us got a spanking and then got washed in lye soap. I guess we scared the hell out of that old White cab driver. I guess he thought, "These people want to integrate? They're still savages." But it was one of the best days of my young life.

* * * * * * * * * * *

Christmas at the Hollow was a magical time during my childhood. Not only did we have the snow to set the mood of the season but riding down the hill on the sleds Poppa made was pure glory.

The Jobbers Pants Company was started by Dr. Dana O. Baldwin, an African American physician, before World War II to produce pants and uniforms for American soldiers. Dr. Baldwin and his partner (Saul Schreibfeder) started the company because White knitting mills refused to hire African American women to work on the production lines. The explanation they gave for not hiring us was so nonsensical it defied reason. Because our nostrils were so large, we would breath in too much lint and it would kill us. Can you imagine? Doretha worked for Jobbers for some time. When I was about eleven, she got laid off from the pants factory when work got short.

Instead of staying in the area and working as a domestic, she and my Aunt Marthy (from my grandfather's side) went to New York where they got jobs as maids. Doretha worked for the family that invented the Chatty Cathy doll. It seemed like Doretha was gone for an eternity.

The best Christmas I can recall as a child was when Doretha made a surprise visit home. It had been snowing heavily that December. Doretha returned home during a severe snowstorm. Somehow she had gotten a ride that dropped her off at the mailbox at the bottom of the hill. She made that mile-long trek up the hill to the Hollow while it was still snowing heavily. When she walked in the door, snow was piled up on her shoulders and on the tan beret she was wearing. The accumulated snow made her look like an angel. It startled all of us. She only had one gift and that was a Chatty Cathy Doll for Christine. I was too much of a tomboy and something like that never would have interested me anyway. The true Christmas gift that year was having my mother home from New York. She stayed with us for about a week before going back. Aunt Marthy had also come home and surprised her family as well.

Another Christmas, a year or so later, Grandma Dollie bought me a chemistry set. It was great and I *loved* it. But being a child, when I showed it to Doretha I told her that I wished Grandma had gotten me the set that included the scale. Doretha looked around to see if Grandma Dollie was nearby. She beckoned me to her, looked me right in the eyes, and said in a near whisper, "Gal, don't you *dare* say anything like that to Dollie. Don't you dare! She paid for this set for more than six months. It cost her more than eighteen dollars. Don't you dare be ungrateful!" My little feelings were crushed that I had been so naïve. I realized that had I made a comment like that to Grandma Dollie it would have hurt her feelings but she never would have let on. I also realized in that second just how much Grandma Dollie loved me to have paid for the set over such a long time. She only averaged about fifteen dollars a week. It was literally more than a week's salary for her to buy the chemistry set for me. I treasured that set for years. It had all but rotted before she or Doretha finally threw it away.

Grandma Dollie was always there for Christmas and the holiday had always been a big deal. The women of the house (Momma Rosie, Grandma Dollie, Wootsie, and eventually Doretha) would decide who would make what. Because Doretha worked at the factory, the workers often received a ham or a turkey, along with a bag of oranges, as a Christmas gift. The women of Koehler Hollow would supplement that gift with other meats.

The kids had to crack black walnuts for Wootsie's mandatory graham cracker cake. That was her specialty. We didn't mind cracking all those walnuts, but they had extremely tough shells. We really had to work hard to get the meat out of those nuts. I still have the recipe and the Bundt cake pan that Wootsie used. I use it every year to make the same cake. Wootsie's other seasonal specialty was chitlins. She obsessed over them. She only made ten pounds and that was it. Those Christmas memories were special.

My Aunt Wootsie was the wildest and most defiant of Poppa and Momma Rosie's seven children. She was worldly and, I must add, loads of fun. She didn't marry until she was fifty-nine years old.

Grandma Dollie's house was empty during the week, so Aunt Wootsie decided to turn it into an informal bootleg joint. We were school age at the time. David, Loretta, Christine and I had just gotten off the bus and were about to make our trek up to the Hollow when we heard a police siren. We all turned around to see what was happening and saw this car barreling around this steep curve up on two wheels. Just as the car got to where we were standing, it dropped back down on all four wheels and kept speeding.

Although the car was moving fast, we all knew the driver was Shadrack Jones, the delivery man for the big White bootleggers. He had a side deal with Wootsie, so we had seen him around the Hollow from time to time. She, however, was small potatoes compared to some of his major clients.

Shadrack was also a talented piano player and was in demand for several area social events. But his main job was delivering bootleg and avoiding capture.

Following Shadrack's speeding car a few seconds behind was Alfred Stegall chasing him in a police car with sirens and lights going full blast. The four of us were standing in amazement looking at each other to make sure everyone saw what had just taken place. Within seconds, it seemed, Shadrack was speeding back by us in the opposite direction, which seemed to defy time and physics. He performed a driving maneuver known regionally as a "bootleg" turn, when a driver being chased makes a quick U-turn on a two-lane road. Shadrack cocked that wheel so fast that the back end of the car swung around and he was speeding in the other direction toward us. Stegall was still moving in the opposite direction from Shadrack. As Shadrack passed us staring right at him in wide-eyed amazement, he tipped his cap to let us know that everything was under control. We all raised our hands simultaneously to wave him on. Of course, Alfred Stegall never caught him. That's why Shadrack was in such demand by the White bootleggers. They knew he wasn't likely to get caught if the police started chasing him. He could negotiate those backwoods roads with the same facility that we had seen him display out on that open road.

* * * * * * * * * * *

Mountain people like us, whether Black or White, were hunters. It was a part of our culture. We hunted rabbits, squirrels, raccoons, groundhogs, and even bears every so often. We also trapped opossums.

A few possums would hang around our house, looking for food no doubt. Sometimes we might come out at night to go to the outhouse and see several possums out scavenging for food. As soon as the lamplight hit them, they would scatter like rats. Once, one fell over and played dead (i.e., played possum), and he ended up getting slaughtered.

At the time, Grandma Dollie worked for the Bassetts and could cook anything from filet mignon to lobster. I didn't know what any of those things were then. One day, Grandma Dollie brought home a small jar with two maraschino cherries. I was wondering what she was going to do with them, because she only had two. I soon found out. My grandmother skinned that possum, baked it, and put one of those cherries in its mouth and baked sweet potatoes around it. It was sitting on a platter in the middle of the table looking like a large pink rat with its eyes gone. It had a little pointy beak and a cherry in its mouth. I want you to know I ate cornbread for dinner that evening, and I was happy to do so. However, my crazy baby brother was just delighted that no one else wanted to eat possum meat. He walked around all evening with possum grease running down his arms looking like Jethro Bodine on *The Beverly Hillbillies*. So, Terry, this story is for you. Of course, I went to bed hungry that night, but I did *not* eat that possum.

2

Amy Finney

I want to tell you more about the Finney family matriarch, my great-great-grandmother Amy. Her determination, perseverance, and grit resulted in the establishment of Koehler Hollow. As an enslaved child growing up on the Mitchell plantation, Amy moved from bringing in the firewood and helping in the kitchen and dining room to working in the fields, which she preferred. I just imagine she found it easier to walk behind a horse or a mule and steady a plow than to stay in the house playing the obsequious servant all day long. That trait does not run well in our family.

As a little girl, I caught all manner of creatures in the woods surrounding Koehler Hollow. Everyone said it was impossible to catch a hummingbird, including Poppa. "It's impossible to catch you a hummn' bird, gal," he said. But I watched and watched those birds and I noticed something about them.

They had to back up to go forward. I thought to myself, "That's pretty cool." I got me a big mouth jar and crept into the flower garden. Momma Rosie's flower garden had every butterfly, every bumblebee, and every hummingbird in the world in it. I held that big mouth jar behind the hummingbird and sure enough, that hummingbird backed into the jar and I closed it. I caught a hummingbird. That's when I realized that I had the knack for watching and observing.

I also caught insects like grasshoppers and bees. But none of them compared to the stately black widow. I developed a morbid curiosity for those spiders.

We had a woodpile near the house for cooking and that pile was full of black widows. Doretha and the other women in the family were afraid of these creatures, but I didn't understand why because I thought they were noble animals. Something about the black widow drew my attention. I thought about how beautiful they were as I observed them. Yes, I had heard that their bite could be poisonous, but that advice was for everyone else, not for a hard-headed, inquisitive child like me who knew better. I decided to start collecting them. I would catch the spiders and then slide a small piece of wood down behind their heads to kill them. Their bodies were so beautiful and shiny. Each one had a different design on its underside than the other. I had several dead spiders in a jar within a short period of time.

One afternoon I was out adding to my black widow collection, and Grandma Dollie came in the yard and saw my jar with about five or six dead black widows in it. Now, Grandma Dollie never scolded me, but when she saw me with these spiders, she spoke to me very harshly. Her eyes widened and she shouted almost at the top of her voice, "What chu' you doin' gal? What chu' doin'? Why'd you have those?" I was frightened by the tone of her voice alone because I had never heard her speak like that before to anyone. I certainly didn't understand why she was so upset with me. Tears were streaming down her face as she grabbed my arm tightly and made me promise I would never, ever catch another black widow in my life. Of course, I promised. But I did so more out of fear and shock at her demeanor.

Before that moment, I had been Grandma's little darling who could do no wrong. When things calmed down, I asked her why I had upset her so by catching these spiders. She sat me down beside her and almost apologetically told me a story that her grandmother had passed on to her when she was no more than ten or eleven.

When Grandma Dollie told me this story about our family matriarch she insisted that I remember what she said. It has been more than sixty-five years since she first told me this story, and I haven't forgotten a word.

During the time of enslavement, her grandmother, Amy, was the property of the Mitchell Plantation in Henry County. Amy had a younger brother named Ben who was no more than four or five at the time. He was a beautiful brown boy with black curly locks. Based on his lighter skin, he was probably Master Mitchell's child with Amy's mother. Ben was what they called a mulatto.

The lady of the plantation, Mistress Mitchell, loved Ben so much that she would sit him on her lap and feed him grapes off the vines of the grape arbor. Grandma Amy thought somewhere deep down, Mistress Mitchell knew Ben was her husband's child.

Well, Master Mitchell hated seeing that little black boy sitting up in his wife's lap. It probably had nothing to do with Ben, but Master Mitchell stayed mad with his wife, because she wouldn't let him have his "field day" down in the slave quarters.

At any rate, Master told his wife, "One of these days dat boy is gon' be in my grape arbor stealin' my grapes 'cause you're givin' 'em to him. When dat happens, I'm gon' whip his ass." That was an unmistakable threat, and everyone who heard him knew it. Mistress Mitchell didn't pay her husband no mind at the time. Ben was so adorable that she carried on loving and spoiling him. Everyone else who heard Master Mitchell's warning, however, held their breath.

As fate would have it, Master Mitchell rode up on his big horse one day and caught little Ben eating grapes off the vines in the arbor. Grandma Amy was carrying water nearby at the time. When the boy saw him, he tried to run, but Master Mitchell caught Ben by the arm and violently jerked him up. He took a log from a woodpile and struck the boy on the leg. Grandma Amy and others in the area heard his little leg break from the blow as Ben screeched in pain. Before Master

Mitchell could strike a second blow, his wife arrived and stopped him. With that single strike, however, Ben was badly injured. Amy dropped the water she was carrying when she heard Ben scream but fought the impulse to run to her little brother's aid. She knew from experience that could have made the situation worse. After Master Mitchell stormed off, his wife signaled Amy to come and tend to her little brother who was still screaming in agony. As Amy carried off her baby brother with tears streaming down his little face, she vowed to herself that she'd get even with old Master Mitchell for harming this child in such a cruel manner.

Amy's primary job on the plantation was to carry the wood and fetch water for the household cook. Even though she was only eleven years old she was a big, strong girl for her age. She encountered lots of black widows in the woodpile while doing her work. Amy had been warned from when she was young to be careful around them because they could be quite poisonous. That's when an idea came to her, and she started collecting the spiders. She gathered several and placed them in a back windowsill of the big house to dry, after she used a small pick to run them through. Once they dried, she ground them as fine as she could. Another of Grandma Amy's jobs in the house was to set the long dinner table for the master and mistress and any other dinner guests they might have. Master Mitchell was typically at one end of the table and the mistress was at the other end. The table was so long that they each had separate sets of salt and pepper shakers. Amy put the bodies of the ground-up black widows in Master Mitchell's pepper shaker. He *loved* to see the pepper falling on his food like dust and Amy dutifully complied.

Grandma Amy fed Master Mitchell the pepper laced with ground black widows for a few weeks before he began showing signs of illness. He became sluggish and ached all over. Sores broke out all over his body and he couldn't sit upright, not even on his prized horse. A doctor was eventually sent for. Back then the doctors used to cut you to bleed out the bad blood. In this case it might have been a good idea because Master Mitchell was poisoned for sure as his health continued to deteriorate. If people had bad or missing teeth, which was likely in the case of the old master, the spider poison could enter the system and affect other parts of the body.

At the end stage of his illness, young Amy said his head had swollen up as big as a foot tub and he couldn't talk much either. Soon after going off to the hospital in North Carolina, word came back to the plantation that Master Mitchell had died. He just died. Amy started feeling bad about things, but she also became worried. She started thinking that somebody might figure out she had poisoned the old man with the dead black widows, so she needed to act remorseful. Grandma Amy said when they went to bury Master Mitchell, she just fell out crying, "Lawd, Lawd, Massa's dead. Massa's *dead*!" She was so "overcome with grief" she just "passed out" and had to be revived. People felt so bad about her reaction to the old man's death. They just believed Amy loved Master so.

After Grandma Dollie told me that story, I had a different kind of respect for black widows. I never harmed one from that day until now. Of course, Amy's little brother Ben was permanently disabled for the remainder of his life because of that physical assault that the old man had carried out against him. He lived to be thirty-seven years old but maintained a noticeable limp from that childhood injury. Amy's youngest son, George, remembered his Uncle Ben from when he was young. In honor of Grandma Amy's little brother, several generations of Finneys have named their sons "Ben."

* * * * * * * * * * *

Amy passed a lot of these stories to her granddaughter, Dollie, who passed them down to me. After Emancipation, she routinely hired herself out as a laborer once she finished working her own land. Her height and size made her a formidable worker. One day she went to work for a White man at a nearby farm. When you're plowing, you have to leave at the crack of dawn with your horses and their harness and get wherever you're going before the sun comes up.

Amy showed up at the farm and plowed to midday in the hot sun right beside the old farmer. When time came for lunch, the old man left the field and went up to the house and started eating lunch up on the porch. Amy could see him, but she kept plowing. She knew she'd be eating soon, because it was the custom for farmers to feed their field hands and temporary workers.

After he finished eating, though, the old man called the dogs. They ran up on the porch, jumped up on the table, and had their fill of the leftovers. After the dogs had eaten, the farmer called for Amy. She dropped that plow right where she stood. She unhooked her horses and made it clear that she didn't intend to do any more work. The old man called out to her, "Gal, gal, where you goin'? Where you goin'? We got more work to do. I was gon' give you somethin' to eat."

"I can eat at home," Amy said. "You turn loose my littl' bit[1] from your'n," she told him.

"Amy, what'd I'do?!"

Grandma Amy walked up to the old farmer and said, "White folks first, dogs second, and niggas last. You turn loose my littl' bit from your'n. I'm goin' home."

The old farmer didn't pay her at first, but with her imposing frame, she stepped up to the man looking down on him and said more firmly, "*You* turn loose my littl' bit from your'n." The old farmer paid her, and she left.

One other time Grandma Amy also had to stare down a White farmer because of a payment dispute. If a woman plowed at all, she typically did so with one horse. But Amy plowed with two, the same as a man. She had her own barn and kept her horses in pristine shape. Amy once took her two horses and plowed land for a White farmer a few miles away.

---

[1] "Bit" was a colloquial expression for "Pay me my money."

She should have received a full day's pay—fifty cents, the same as a man. At the end of the day, Amy went to the farmer for payment, and he gave her twenty-five cents. She looked down at the quarter and told him, "I works jes lek a man, I gits paid lek a man." The farmer said, "Gal, you' a woman. A woman don't get paid same as a man," whereupon Amy laid hands on him and grabbed him by the collar and repeated, "Leks I said, I works lek a man, I gits paid lek a man." The farmer gave her the other twenty-five cents. She didn't worry about any repercussions because the White farmer would have been too ashamed to let anyone know that a Black woman had stared him down, much less jacked him up. She got her money and was off.

The only time Grandma Amy was less smart with her money was when she married for the second time in 1883. This man, Peter Ramey, who was from Patrick County, was apparently a real slickster. He was a light-skinned man and a dapper dresser. He apparently duped Amy out of her money before running off, or at least that's the way the story was told. Poppa recalled that she ran him off after discovering he had spent her money. Either way, she wasn't to be trifled with.

Grandma Amy's willingness to work hard made it possible for her to accomplish what many men couldn't. By plowing other farmers' fields in addition to working her own, she was able to accumulate enough money to expand her original acre. She bought her own land in 1890, and by the mid-1890s she owned it free and clear. It remains in our family today.

Amy continued to thrive mostly through her wits into the twentieth century. She was hard to pigeonhole. She became quite renowned in these parts as a midwife. Grandma Dollie believed her grandmother delivered or cared for more than 150 babies in her time. She was also a master herbalist. I didn't learn until I was an adult that in addition to her other talents, she was a highly regarded cook. The Hotel Roanoke hired her as their head cook.

During the influenza epidemic of the late 1910s, Grandma Amy delivered babies as her main source of income. In fact, she was renowned for her midwifery skills in Henry and Franklin counties. She also developed a cure for childbed fever.[2] Women came down with it because of unsanitary conditions before and just after childbirth. It was not uncommon for some women to die in tremendous pain from that infection. Amy was able to heal those infections with a concoction of roots and herbs she put together. Blacks and Whites (most of them husbands) came from miles around to get Amy Finney to deliver their babies.

Her cure for childbed fever spread around the area and made her a minor celebrity. A White doctor who practiced in the area was known to have said he didn't know anything about Black people because we weren't the same anatomically

---

[2] It was also known as puerperal fever or simply as puerperal infection. It was contracted in the vaginal area during and after childbirth or miscarriage. If left untreated, it could be fatal.

as Whites. Therefore he refused to "doctor" on us. The same doctor had once been asked to see a little Black boy who had dislocated his shoulder and had also broken his hip, but he refused to treat him. Everybody in the community knew about this doctor's views, including Grandma Amy. He had, however, heard about her cure for childbed fever. He decided to come up to Koehler Hollow to get this cure from the ignorant, old Colored woman.

He rode up onto her land in his buckboard. Grandma Amy was sitting on her front porch smoking her corncob pipe, rocking in her chair with her long dress below her knees just above her ankles. He just pulled up to her porch on his buggy without getting out. He just looked at her and said, "You Amy Finney?" Grandma looked at him and responded, "Aapp."

"I hear tell you got a cure for dat d'ere childbed fever and I'm here to get it. I hear dat cure of yours is workin'." Grandma studied him for a minute. Then she asked,

"Is you a doctor?"

"I am."

"So, you can read?"

"Well of course, I can read."

"And write?"

"Yes, I can write too," he said a little impatiently.

"And cipher[3] too?"

---

[3] To count

"Yes, I can do all those things, gal. So, tell me how I can get dat cure from you."

Grandma Amy said, "Hmp. If you can read, write, and cipher, you figure it out." She leaned back in her chair, put her pipe back in her mouth and stared right through that doctor and never spoke another word. The man got the message. That doctor rode off in his buggy right along with his ignorance and his arrogance right out of Koehler Hollow. In retrospect, it might have been a good idea for her to give it to him since she knew she would never get any credit for it. But there was no need to make that doctor rich.

When I went to DuPont in 1976, I met a fellow employee, a White woman who was in her sixties at the time. She asked me, "Who are your people?" That is a Southern tradition to understand who you were and where you had come from. I told her I was a Finney on my mother's side. She quickly volunteered in her thick Southern drawl, "I was named after a Colored woman named Amy Finney. She was my momma's midwife, and I was told she kept me and my momma alive when I was a baby."

"Well, that was my great-great-grandmother."

"Well, I'll be darn." A lot of the problems I had been having at that job went away after this woman spread the news of who my folks were. It was as if Grandma Amy had come back and blessed me from beyond.

* * * * * * * * * * *

By the late 1920s, Grandma Amy had left Virginia and was living in Cleveland, Ohio, with her son King Finney who had moved away years earlier and established himself there. She moved there to help him after his wife Annie and their daughter died in childbirth. Amy affirmed that had she been there, she would have delivered her granddaughter with no trouble.

Amy loved her third son, but the two often clashed. They typically butted heads over King's womanizing. Amy didn't like it and didn't hesitate to express her disapproval of him running with so many women after his wife's death. She wanted King to remarry, settle down with one woman (preferably one she approved of), and have children.

Things between those two came to a head when Amy told one of King's girlfriends he had been with another woman just the day before. When the girlfriend confronted King, they got in a huge brawl and she tried to cut him. When the girlfriend blurted out she found out about his infidelity from his mother, King was furious with Amy. In fact, it sealed a proper breach in their mother/son relationship. King was so angry with his mother that he put her out of his place. He put her on a train back to Virginia and told her he never wanted to see her again. King then wrote a letter to Poppa telling him what Amy had done. He said not only did he not want to see Grandma Amy again, according to Poppa, King told him to not even bother about telling him when she died. The family lost touch with King pretty much after that. We have no further information about what happened to him.

Poppa and his wife Momma Rosie settled Grandma Amy back in her house at the bottom of the hill. Sometime in the early 1930s, after returning from Ohio, Grandma Amy suffered a stroke and couldn't walk without assistance. She eventually became all but bedridden. Every morning, however, Momma Rosie went down to Amy's house and tended to her. Amy had never particularly liked her daughter-in-law, but Momma Rosie looked after her, nonetheless, because Amy was her husband's mother and it was the right thing for her to do.

Doretha was a child when Amy came back from Cleveland, but she was old enough at eight years old to take on the responsibility of looking after her grandmother in the morning. Doretha and Uncle Sunny Boy went down in the morning to make a fire, brought in water for her grandmother, and emptied her slop jar. Then she would go back to the main house and bring down Amy's breakfast and perform any other chores that needed to be done.

While Doretha was doing her chores, Amy would tell Uncle Sunny Boy to get in the bed with her and keep warm. He was no more than five and probably wouldn't have been of much help anyway. The old woman said he shouldn't do "womenfolks" work. But Mother resented the old lady. So, to spite Grandma Amy, Mother would dance the hoochie choochie, swaying her little hips for Grandma Amy to see. Sometimes she would sing blues songs that she had heard at Uncle Ramey and Aunt Alice's juke joint. Amy would become so agitated when Doretha did this she would throw things at her calling her a little "fawd" hussy. Sometimes, Amy would try to hit Doretha with her cane, but Mother swung her hips and taunted the old lady just outside her reach. Doretha would sway her hips right out the door, laughing all the way.

Grandma Amy died on July 6, 1936, at around eighty-six years old. True to his word, her son King did not show up for his mother's funeral, but Amy's other children came back to funeralize their mother. Grandma Dollie remembered the funeral quite well. She recalled the minister saying something about losing another person of Grandma Amy's generation who had lived through enslavement in this part of the world. Grandma Dollie said the preacher commented that before long, all of those who could give live testimony to the horrors of that experience in the South would soon be gone. He said it was the younger generation's responsibility to keep the memory of Amy and her contemporaries alive. He also said they had to fight any efforts to set our people back. Grandma Dollie took the preacher's words to heart which is why she did her part to maintain Grandma Amy's stories. Despite the fact that the country was in the midst of a depression, Poppa, his brother Ben, and his sister Susan put together the money to buy a headstone for their mother. Her son King remained in Cleveland and died there in the 1940s.

Not long after Amy's death, her only daughter, Susan, Poppa's sister, also died. 1936 was a tough year for the family.

3

George Finney

Ge300 eorge Washington Finney, as I have said, was an honorable man. All of his life we called him "Poppa," because he was a father to his children, to his grandchildren, and to his great-grandchildren—including Christine, David, Loretta, and me.

As a boy, George only made it as far as the third grade. He loved to run and play hopscotch. He had two older brothers and a sister. When Grandma Amy made them leave the house for school, his brother Ben would get about two-thirds of the way there, put his book in a tree trunk, and tell Poppa, "I'll see you bro'. I ain't goin' in der." Then he'd be off to play. Poppa, on the other hand, went to school for as long as he could.

Sitting in front of the potbelly stove in the bedroom, Poppa told us how he did not have a pair of trousers until he was eight years old. All he wore was a guano sack. It was one of those huge coarse cloth bags that animal feed and fertilizer came in. Holes were cut at the bottom end of the sack for his head to go through and on the side for his arms to stick out. It was sewn at the bottom with a tie around the waist so he wouldn't look like he was wearing a dress. Poppa said the worst day of the year was when he got a new guano sack because it stung and itched until it was broken in. He said it was an "abomination" to have it on your skin. I could hardly imagine little George Finney walking barefoot with his books to school wearing a guano sack.

As an adult, Poppa was a tall slender man with a high hairline. He was a beautiful shade of brown with totally clear skin. When he was a teenager, Poppa lost his right eye when he was chopping wood and a piece struck him in the eye. Even though he only had one eye, he wore reading glasses. He would put his artificial eye in its socket on Sundays, sometimes. But he otherwise kept it in a matchbox. Kissing Poppa was like kissing sticker briars because his whiskers were so sharp. So, we waited until he shaved on Sunday and all the girls would stand in line to kiss him. That way you didn't get stuck when you put your lips close to his face.

Poppa wore bib overalls and chewed a clove of garlic every day. When he walked, you could hear him coming from a distance as those overalls made a swish, swish, swish sound. His feet didn't point straight, which made his movement slightly awkward. Poppa read the Bible every night beside the old potbelly stove in the bedroom. Sometimes he'd be called on to preach from the pulpit.

He kept a watch in his pocket. In the evening, we would often crawl up into his lap and just listen to his watch. I can still remember David sitting on his lap listening to his watch in front of that potbelly stove.

Poppa was a very smart man. Even with his third-grade education, he could do algebra. Because he could cipher,[1] he taught us math. He taught us to say "alt" instead of zero. Of course by 1957, the teachers weren't saying "alt" anymore, but we continued to do so at home. I hope I have his integrity. At least I try to. That man who wore the guano sack as a child and paid poll taxes in order to vote in this county set a high-water mark for me and everyone else in our family even in the twenty-first century.

****

Poppa and Momma Rosie had several sons and daughters. Grandma Dollie was the second youngest. They had a son, James Cabel Finney, who was born in 1905, and a grandson, William, who was called "Reely," who they also raised as their son. Uncle James routinely caught the train from the Koehler Station to go to Bassett where he worked in a furniture factory. On Sunday afternoon, September 6, 1931, James had an early

---

[1] Basic math

shift Monday morning and ran to catch the train to Bassett. He had intended to stay overnight at his brother Ramey's place.

James was running late and missed the train at the Koehler stop. He managed to cut across the hill and caught up with it as it slowed down around the curve. He got on the train in the middle of the segregated car so he had to make his way back to the section where the Black people sat. As he did so, he met a White conductor who challenged him for being in the wrong section. The two had words, and the conductor manhandled Uncle James. He managed to grab James and threw him off the moving train. That White conductor killed Uncle James right in front of the shocked White onlookers!

The medical examiner ruled that the "deceased came to his death by falling from a moving railroad car and receiving a fractured skull . . . death was instantaneous." In other words, it was ruled an accident, despite several White witnesses who swore Uncle James had not resisted and the conductor simply threw the young man off the train.

Poppa was devastated when he heard what had happened. The county's entire Black community was outraged by the atrocity. James was the son of the highly respected "Mr. Finney." It was as if Poppa's leadership position in the community and an elder in the church translated into some level of respect for his whole family and they were under pressure to uphold it publicly. The irony is that Uncle James was just trying to get to the back of the train following the segregation codes of the period.

After burying Uncle James, Poppa decided to sue the Norfolk Western Railroad Line for killing his son. He wanted to take out criminal charges against the conductor who threw his son from the train, but the courts would not allow that because Uncle James' death had been ruled an "accident." In any case, the wrongful death lawsuit was allowed to proceed.

Poppa didn't use a lawyer. He just used his common sense and told the judge that his son was only trying to get to the back of the train where he was supposed to ride. The conductor was called to the stand. The closest he came to apologizing to Poppa was when he said he was sorry for how things turned out that day. It was not an admission of guilt or culpability. The judge upheld the accidental death ruling, but also ruled that Norfolk Western be held responsible for Uncle James' death. He ordered the railroad line to pay the $11 court cost. He also ordered the railroad company to compensate Poppa for the loss of his son, but the amount was kept out of the official record. Family lore put the assessed amount between $450 and $500. It was a large sum at the time, but it was hardly enough to replace his son. When Poppa received the check, he was also informed that Norfolk Western had terminated the conductor involved.

When Poppa told that story years later, tears welled up in his eyes. He said he had expected Uncle James to follow him as a community leader, but his life was cut short.

* * * * * * * * * * *

Grandma Amy realized early on that her youngest child, George, would be her most stable and, as it turned out, most reliable child. Although Poppa and his siblings were raised in Amy's small cottage on the property, he had ambitions for a much larger dwelling for his family, which prompted him to build the main house at Koehler Hollow in 1924.

Back in Poppa's early years, the workday lasted from sunup to sundown. In the early 1920s, before he built his house in the Hollow, Poppa and Momma Rosie lived in the Veneer Hollow in Bassett, where he worked in the Veneer plant. But in the evenings after quitting time, he would head off to Koehler with planks of wood that he bought from the plant to build his house. It still stands today at 100 years old. Doretha was the first of their grandchildren born in that house in 1927. Every plank and board was put there by George Washington Finney. The two chimneys in that house were built with his two hands.

When the Great Depression came and everybody wanted for jobs, Poppa was working at the Veneer plant. He was one of the two Black workers there who could read and write. One day his foreman told him, "George, we gotta cut your pay from a dollar a day to fifty cents." Poppa looked the man square in the face and said, "A man don't work for less than a dollar a day." The foreman responded, "Times 'a hard here George. Seventy-five cents is the best I can do." "I won't be back," Poppa said. He quit and went home to farm. He was able to support his family through farming and bartering, and carpentry and Momma Rosie assisted by taking in laundry.

Before he quit working at the plant, Poppa told us about this young Black man who also worked at the Veneer plant. One of Poppa's favorite pastimes was chewing sweet tobacco. The very fragrance of it reminds me of him even today. This younger man came to Poppa one day and asked him, "Uncle George, can I have a chew of tobacky?" It only cost a nickel to buy a plug,[2] Poppa cut him off a chew and handed it to him. The next day the same guy came again and asked Poppa for a chew of "bacca." Poppa cut him off a piece and handed it to him. The third day when the man came back for another chew, Poppa reached into his pocket, handed him a nickel and said, "Here'n. You take dis' here nickel and go buy you your own chew. And don't ask me for nan other chew 'til I ask you for one. It's unbecomin' for a grown man t'a go 'round beggin'."

During the Depression, Poppa always asked Momma Rosie to bake more bread than was needed, because according to him, "You don't never know when a fella is gon' come by here hungry. It ain't fittin' for somebody to come by yo' house and you can't offer 'em at least some bread and a little jelly." There was always extra bread in the cupboard for that very reason.

* * * * * * * * * * *

---

[2] A bite-size, pressed mass of chewing tobacco.

Poppa's case against the Norfolk Western Railroad Line wasn't the only time he found himself in court before a judge. He went to court at least one other time because he refused to be bullied and treated as a second-class citizen when he knew his rights.

Poppa had contracted with this White man to allow him to go across his property, which he had expanded to several acres by then, to cut some wood. In return for allowing this, once he was finished, the man would give Poppa the sawdust from the cuttings and a sum of money. The White man worked in the area for several months. When all the work was completed, the man started to pull his equipment out. Poppa went down the road and asked for his money. The White man called him an "uppity nigger" and told him he wasn't giving Poppa a damn thing. George Finney just left the scene without saying another word.

Once again, Poppa put on his suit and went uptown took out a warrant and sued this man who had taken the trees from his property without paying him the agreed-upon compensation. Sometime later, Poppa and this White man ended up facing each other in court. The judge asked the man, "Did you make an agreement with Uncle George here to cut trees on his land and in return you'd give him some branches, sawdust, and a piece of money?" The man said, "Yes sir, I did, y'honor. But he's an uppity nigger and didn't 'proach me right." The judge said, "That's not acceptable. You're gonna pay this man. He had a right to ask you for his money." The judge struck his gavel on the block and said, "End of case." The man had to pay and Poppa won in court again.

* * * * * * * * * * *

How Black people endured and lived in the repressive, segregated region of Appalachia has been misrepresented. If they depict us at all, Hollywood has us all fearful, broke down, and demeaned with hat in hand. That is not my recollection or experience in the South before integration. My great-grandfather, George Finney, walked with his head held high. He was a proud man. Our White neighbors, however, would not call him "Mr. Finney" because it took too much to give respect to a Black man. But George Washington Finney was truly "Mr. Finney," even though the whites called him "Uncle George." African Americans in the area *always* called him "Mr. Finney," or oftentimes "Mister George."

We had no immediate neighbors up in the Hollow. By the time I was born, we had two houses. The cottage belonging to Grandma Amy was long gone. At one point in the 1950s we rented to a White family named the Davises. Can you imagine that? Whites paying rent to a Black man in the 1950s. We were friends with their kids. When we were young, we would have the best fights. We would chunk[3] rocks at them and they chunk rocks at us. It was a miracle that none of us got any serious injuries from these fights. I mean we would stoop and get a rock and fling it as hard as we could. Sometimes you might

---

[3] Throw

get hit, but most times you didn't. Mud was the best thing to throw. Hard clay from the garden was also good because it would just shatter when it hit things.

In 1958, Poppa went to Appalachian Power to ask them to put electricity in our house and they turned him down. Our White renters went to the same company shortly after Poppa and made the same request because someone had given them an electric stove. Sure enough, they came to the Hollow to put in the power pole at the White renter's house. Since they were already there, the workers said they would also put electricity into our house. Prior to that, I had done my first, second, and third grade homework by kerosene lamps.

* * * * * * * * * * *

Poppa dutifully paid a poll tax in order to vote all of his life. A lot of people don't know about poll taxes. They were functionally a vehicle for suppressing Black voters. Modern generations have seen the emergence of voter ID laws across the country to keep Black folks from casting their ballots. Voter suppression was standard in the South when I was young. Poor Black people couldn't see any reason for paying to vote, so they didn't. When my late husband, Bill Muse, came to the area in 1946, there were only eleven Black people voting in all of Henry County. George Washington Finney was at the top of that list.

I remember as a little kid in the early 1960s, Poppa would don his suit, put on his hat, get out his walking stick, and go vote on Election Tuesday. He also brought five dollars to pay the required poll tax. He was a proud and resolute Republican. I remember the arguments in our house when Doretha announced that she was voting for John F. Kennedy—a Democrat! Poppa was so upset. "We's 'Publicans!" he said forcefully. "Don'cha know who freed the slaves? We's 'Publicans!" How the Republican Party has changed. Little did Poppa know that the 1960s would begin the transformation of the Republican Party. I'm not sure he'd recognize it were he still alive.

* * * * * * * * * * *

We grew up in Koehler Hollow in the early 1950s with Poppa and Momma Rosie dutifully watching over their brood. One day, we were sitting on our front porch and saw some young White kids come across our property, go into our blackberry patch, and start picking blackberries. David, Loretta, and I wanted to go down the hill and run them off. Poppa, who always spoke very slowly said, "Nap, just hold up a bit." Poppa kept watching them from the front porch. David and I kept an eye on them as they picked and picked. Just when they appeared to be ready to leave the blackberry patch, Poppa said, "Gwon' in dat d'ere kitchen an' fetch me a bucket." We did as he told us. Poppa stepped off the front porch, walked down the hill, and stopped those two young kids. He said,

"Y'all chillun know d'is here is private property?" One of the kids said,

"Ye'suh. We jes' come here to get some of these black-berries."

"But dey not yo' blackberries. Dey mine and you didn't ask me to pick 'em. So han' 'em here."

He made them dump the berries into the bucket we came with. He then told them, "Now you git off my property and remember—you don't never come on a man's property and take nothin' lessen you ask." On top of all that, Poppa got those berries picked without lifting a finger.

Doretha talked about when she was a child during the Great Depression, the hobos, White and Black, would wander up to the Hollow from the train tracks below. The White ones would say to Poppa, "Uncle, I'll cut some wood for you if you give me somethin' to eat." Poppa would respond, "I don't let no man handle my axe." Then he would say, "Rosa, go down in de kitchen and make dat man somethin' to eat." Momma Rosie would go and make some jelly biscuits and get some fat-back and give it to them. They'd always tip their hat and say, "Much obliged," and go on.

Poppa was a Christian man, and no one was supposed to leave his house hungry according to him. He routinely said, "No one should come to dis' here house and not have some-thin' offered to 'em." That was the way he was raised and how he raised us.

Poppa was also a man of the Bible. In fact, he was the most honest man I have ever known. I had more respect for him than any other person in my life.

His wife, Momma Rosie, was as close to an angel as I have ever seen. I never knew any woman to be as sweet, kind, and soft-spoken. Her hands felt like velvet. She too read the Bible every evening. Using the tip of a toothpick, she would point to each word to help us to read the book. These were our earliest reading lessons. The Beatitudes (Matthew 5: 1–12) was her favorite Gospel. She also sat beside that potbelly stove with Poppa and sang,

> "Rock of Ages, cleft for me,
> Let me hide myself in thee . . . "

One day, Poppa took me with him down to Billy Via's store. It was a nice little walk and I always enjoyed him holding my hand as we walked. It gave me such a feeling of security. We always carried a basket and never needed a paper bag. On this one occasion, Poppa paid Billy Via what he owed him for our groceries, but the store owner miscounted and gave Poppa eleven cents too much. Poppa looked at it and said, "Mr. Via, I think you don' made a mistake. You' give me 'leven cents mo' than I was due." Poppa then pushed the eleven cents back across the counter. There was a White customer in the store behind Poppa. Mr. Via was too ashamed to have a Black man count better than him in public. So he said, "No sir, Uncle George. I gave you the right change." "No, suh. Dat's yo' 'leven cents," Poppa said, "I don't take what I don't earn. D'ats yours." He pushed it back and we walked out of the store. I looked back at Mr. Via and his face had turned beet red with embarrassment. Now that eleven cents could have bought me and my brother and sisters some popsicles. But I was prouder of Poppa for sending that eleven cents back across that counter than I would have ever been eating a dozen popsicles. George Finney's favorite expressions were "An honest day's work for an honest day's pay" and "My word is my bond."

* * * * * * * * * * *

I have told you how he looked, about his moral character, how he lived, and about the values he left for us. Now, I must tell you how this heroic man died. It was not an easy time for our family for several reasons.

By the mid-1960s, when the War on Poverty was declared by the Johnson administration, the welfare department began going out to rural counties like ours looking for people who qualified for public assistance. I can remember one day we were sitting on the porch when we saw a car coming up our long dirt road to the Hollow. A cloud of dust flying up always announced a car's arrival before it was visible.

A White woman got out of the car, dressed in a uniform with a military-like hat. She walked very purposefully up the hill. Poppa and Momma Rosie were sitting in their rocking chairs swaying back and forth in unison and watching their great-grandchildren. The lady came to the porch and asked in a proper Southern accent, "Are you Mr. Finney?"

"Yes'm."

"Well, I'm from the welfare department and it has come to our attention that your family qualifies for public assistance."

"Now what's dis' here public 'sistance?"

"When families are below the poverty level and they need help in feeding their children. We are here to help in that endeavor," she said. He looked around after we had resumed playing in the yard, and not one of us showed the slightest sign of malnutrition.

"It is a poor man that can't feed his chillun," Poppa said.

"But Mr. Finney, you don't understand . . . . ,"

"Much obliged, ma'am, but we don't need none of yo' 'sistance," he interjected. "I do thank you very much, though." He tipped his hat, nodded politely, and turned his face from the woman and got back to rocking in unison with Momma Rosie, who never stopped her chair and never uttered a word. I don't think she even looked in the woman's direction.

I remember the expression on the White woman's face. She just turned around and walked down the hill to her car. It was one of the greatest days of my life, because I knew what Poppa had done for his great-grandkids' self-esteem. I knew the children who got welfare at school, and they were made fun of because they had taken handouts. I never wanted that label and Poppa made sure that neither I nor any of my brother or sisters had to have it.

Poppa passed away after another tragedy in our family. That's when we also lost my sister Loretta. It was the Wednesday afternoon before Thanksgiving and there was general commotion in the main house. Momma Rosie, Dollie, and Wootsie were all occupied preparing some part of the Thanksgiving meal. Doretha was doing laundry. I was helping her with that and babysitting my youngest brother, Terry, who was about three then. David, Loretta, Christine, and I had scraped together some money to go down to Fatty Oates' store to buy some candy. Even though David was a year older me, I had always been the responsible one, because I was the oldest daughter, and I was expected to look after the younger ones. It never dawned on me to not let David, who was fourteen and the oldest of the three, take Loretta and Christine, because at twelve and eleven years old the girls were not babies. Besides, it was a routine trip to the store. I have kicked myself a thousand times for not going with them.

They went to the store and got the candy and were coming back home when the train was also approaching on the tracks. David, unwilling to wait for the train to pass, yelled to Loretta and Christine, "Let's run before the train gits here," and darted across the track. Loretta made sure Christine got across, because she was the slowest, and then she attempted to outrun the train. She almost made it, but the handle rail on the side of the train that the conductor used to get on and off board, struck her on the side of her head with such force that it killed her instantly. She was knocked about ten feet from where the train had hit her. The freight train conductor saw the kids running across the tracks and realized the train had struck Loretta. He immediately brought the train to a halt.

David and Christine made it back to the house. He was half-crying and breathlessly informed Doretha of the accident. He was talking so fast and so incoherently that she couldn't follow what he was saying at first. When she understood what had happened, Doretha let out a high-pitched wail. It was as if that scream lingered in the air on a single note for more than a minute. It was so piercing. I have never forgotten that sound all these years. I was holding Terry at the time and nearly dropped him when Doretha screamed. He started crying in response to her screech. In my gut I knew what had happened and dropped to my knees in prayer asking the Lord to please let it not be true.

When I made it to David, he was still crying, but Christine looked like she was in a daze. She must have been in shock. The moment I didn't see Loretta with them, I knew something terrible had happened to my sister. I put the baby down and started running in the direction of the train. I was chasing Doretha, who was already out the door and moving fast in the same direction. I kept saying in my mind, "Please God. Don't let it be true. Don't let it be true."

By the time we made it to the tracks, the train had stopped. Several people had gotten off and were standing around Loretta's body. But there was nothing they could do other than witness. Doretha made it to the scene and immediately started screaming, "My baby!! My baby!! My baby!!" People,

Black and White, moved out of her way so she could get to Loretta. When I made it to the scene, I could only stare at my sister's dead body in total disbelief. Doretha held Loretta close to her chest swaying back and forth as she cried uncontrollably. Loretta's lifeless body simply swung like a ragdoll. Blood had also run out of her nose and ears.

Eventually, an ambulance arrived. The attendants placed Loretta on a stretcher but did not cover her face with the sheet which would have clearly signaled she was dead. I concluded that was a good sign. She was not totally gone, and I had a slight glimmer of hope. I wanted to go in the ambulance with Doretha, but she made me go back home and let everyone there know that she had gone to the hospital. Aunt Wootsie had stayed behind with Momma Rosie, Poppa, and the other kids.

That walk back to the Hollow seemed like it took an eternity. I could feel every step I took. When I made it back, Poppa and Momma Rosie were sitting in their respective rocking chairs and were swaying much faster than usual. Their eyes were closed tight, but tears were streaming down both their faces. Neither Poppa nor Momma said a word. They just rocked in those chairs in unison. Neither of them looked in my direction. Terry had settled down, but even at three years old, he sensed something tragic had taken place. I don't know where Christine and David had gotten to, but I know I couldn't find either of them in the house. Wootsie just sat in the downstairs kitchen. She just stared quietly as if she were in total disbelief.

Sometime later, people started arriving at the house to express condolences. Mr. Clyde, a White neighbor, was the first to arrive. A few others came and brought us food, which is still a Southern custom. Within hours, more arrived at the Hollow. Even though there was plenty of food, nobody ate. It was a solemn atmosphere. This was even more remarkable because the Wednesday before Thanksgiving, people were usually home preparing their family feast.

Poppa, who had already been ailing at that point, had to be admitted back in the hospital a few days after Loretta's death. He was not well enough to attend the funeral.

There was a visitor, a man, who came two or three days after Loretta's death. David, Christine, and I were sent away when he came. We eavesdropped on the conversation but could only make out parts of what was said. He cried and said something about Loretta, but we couldn't make out all of it. Whoever it was and whatever was said really upset Doretha, because she was hurling curse words at him at the top of her voice. She had to be sedated following that visit. Whoever it was and whatever was said was another one of those family issues not spoken of.

I didn't go to my sister's funeral either because of my asthma. Grandma Dollie thought I might get too upset and start having an attack, so I just stayed back at the house. Loretta's funeral was packed with children from her class, and other kids from the school. Her current and former teachers were also there. Later, Christine told me that "Come Ye Disconsolate" was sung during communion. For years, it upset her to hear that song.

My sister's little body was laid to rest up on Mountain Top Cemetery, where Grandma Amy and several of our family are also buried. Eventually, Doretha suffered a nervous breakdown and for a while had to be institutionalized.

We didn't discuss Loretta's death much. We just didn't do that then. This is the most I have said about it since it happened sixty years ago. We were already in hell, what else was there to say? What was talking about it going to do?

Loretta's death has stuck with many of us for better than half a century. As I said, Doretha had to be institutionalized following her child's death. For years on the anniversary of Loretta's passing she would lock herself up in Dollie's house and not speak to anyone. She didn't answer the telephone or have any social interaction. Other family members also experienced panic attacks around that time, including Christine. After years of experiencing these episodes and being afraid to venture out on that tragic day, Christine, now an ordained pastor, called those fears out. Being a God-fearing woman, she stood up to those negative feelings and refused to be ruled by them. She is a heroic woman.

I have never spoken before about one occurrence concerning Loretta's death. Part of me just didn't want to deal with it, but I am telling it here for the first time. The evening before Loretta died, our dog, Rennie, who was a mix of a Collie and a Lab, began howling. This was unusual behavior for him. He was normally a relatively calm dog otherwise, but suddenly he began screeching. It sounded like someone had been torturing him. Christine and Loretta stayed over at Grandma Dollie's house that night. Rennie walked right behind them, howling all the way to Grandma's house. Even after they were inside, Rennie just continued making noises from outside. His wailing unnerved the girls so much that they got in the bed together and clung to each other for protection. At one point, Rennie came around to the bedroom window where they were and continued his wail. Late into the night his howl became more like a soft moan like he was in pain or agony.

I have long believed animals have heightened senses and can see (or at least perceive) things that humans can't. After Christine described this to me, I believe that Rennie saw the death angel hovering near Loretta. Rennie was attempting to warn Loretta and Christine as they walked down the hill to Grandma Dollie's house. The night of Loretta's death and thereafter, Rennie never made another sound. In fact, no one ever heard that distinctive howl from him ever again.

The following month of December also turned out to be a devastating time for our family. Poppa wasn't doing well. He had received a prostate cancer diagnosis and was on the decline. He had been in and out of the hospital between Martinsville and the University of Virginia Medical Center. The shock of Loretta's death surely pushed him to a more vulnerable state. When Doretha screamed at the news, he knew something had happened to one of his great-grandbabies. Poppa never came back home after being admitted to the hospital after Loretta's death. Grandma Dollie, Wootsie, and Momma Rosie went to see him, but back in those days they didn't let kids visit patients in hospitals. On Wednesday December 9, Wootsie came home to tell us that Poppa had died. It was just fourteen days after Loretta's death. Wootsie was stoic when she told us about it. What she said was Poppa wasn't coming home anymore. By then, Christine had come out of her shock and was just as inconsolable as I was.

Momma Rosie helped us through the process by explaining that Poppa's departure was God's will. And just as she was certain that she would see him again, so would we. Momma Rosie said she had been married to him for fifty-nine years, had had his children, and had built a life with him. She told us if anyone had a right to cry and break down it should be her. After all, she said, she felt his absence more keenly than we did. She understood our grief, but told us we would survive it, because Poppa wouldn't have had it any other way. Momma Rosie said Poppa was an old man who had lived a long life. What she said, however, wasn't that comforting. Poppa had been more than our great-grandfather. He had been our protector and our source of knowledge. He taught us all kinds of survival strategies about living in the woods. Poppa taught several of us how to read and do math and was as strong a role model for us as any child could have. And I forgot to mention that he was also a wonderful artist. I still have some of his paintings.

His funeral was also a large one. In fact, Meadow View AME Church had an overflow crowd. Many would-be attendees didn't get inside the building. "Mr. George Washington Finney" had been a pillar of the community—an elder of the church and one of the area's most respected Black citizens. All of his sons and daughters were there. People brought so much food there was no place to store it. Many White neighbors came to pay their respects, as "Uncle George" was also well known to them. They, too, brought food over after his death.

We met cousins that we didn't really know. The Hollow was filled with people. A few of my uncles had to set up tents to accommodate relatives who had traveled in for the funeral. I remember there being a lot of testimonials for him. People stood up and talked about how Poppa had helped them out of this or that crisis. Some people came up to Momma Rosie and handed her money saying they had owed Poppa for some assistance he had given but they hadn't made it around to paying what they owed.

Grandma Dollie kept me with her throughout the funeral because she didn't want me to have an asthma attack without being ready to respond. When one occurred, she gave me a combination of bootleg and hot coffee. The hot coffee stopped the asthma attack and the bootleg relaxed and put me to sleep. It worked like a charm and settled me down every time. That concoction was all I ever had until I was in college when Primatene Mist came out with an over-the-counter inhaler.

It took everyone a while to adjust to our new family reality. For us kids, Koehler Hollow without Poppa was like a church without a minister. There were all kinds of reminders of him around that property. It became a very different place.

For years, I hated celebrating Thanksgiving and Christmas. Loretta's death the day before Thanksgiving and Poppa's death just fourteen days later caused that year's Christmas to be totally dispirited. We had no decorations up and Loretta and Poppa's pictures were draped in black to show we were a family in mourning.

I didn't stop hating Thanksgiving and especially Christmas until I was at St. Paul's Episcopal Church years later. The vicar at the church had a young daughter, Ashley, who favored Loretta. She had been cast to play Mary, the mother of Jesus, in the Christmas play. Her mother and daddy brought her to my house to practice her lines for the play. She would come in the house beaming, and so excited about Christmas. Somehow the wonderment and marvel of the season in that child's eyes softened my heart. How could I hate this holiday and teach little Ashley her part in the Christmas play? Without knowing it, that little girl saved me. I'm not sure she understood why I started crying as she read her lines, so I had to explain to her how I had lost my younger sister and great-grandfather around that time twenty-seven years earlier. I think letting go of that grief at forty years old was one of the healthiest things I have ever done.

4

Momma Rosie

Anyone who wants an idea of what Momma Rosie looked like should look at my sister Christine. Momma Rosie had the prettiest chocolate face with a beautiful smile. Momma Rosie was a small, dark-skinned woman with tiny feet and soft hands. She had the sweetest eyes and the gentlest smile. When we were young, we played with Momma Rosie's hands because they were so soft. We played with the veins on the back of her hands by just running our fingers across them. When she removed her bonnet, her fine shoulder-length hair was as white as snow. By the time we came along, she had developed cataracts, so there was a blue film on her eyes. When she read the Bible, she'd use a toothpick and place the point under every word as she read it aloud. Her favorite section was the Beatitudes from the Book of Matthew. She slowly read:

> "Blessed are the poor in spirit,
> for theirs is the kingdom of heaven.
>
> Blessed are they who mourn,
> for they shall be comforted.
>
> Blessed are the meek,
> for they shall inherit the earth."

We were spellbound when she read. I have those verses memorized today because of her.

Poppa's wife, Rosa Bell Waller Finney, or "Momma Rosie," was George Finney's third cousin. But when you lived in the country at that time, you didn't have a whole lot of options as to whom you could to marry. If you didn't have a car or a horse, you had to find somebody to court within walking distance. That said, Poppa and Momma Rosie were married to each other until the day George Finney passed away. They had a wonderful marriage. I never heard them fuss or spat once.

Poppa's mother, Grandma Amy, did not like Momma Rosie. Because Amy was six foot tall, she thought her son should have married a taller woman. Momma Rosie stood no taller than five feet in her shoes. I think that Amy really didn't like Momma Rosie because, unlike her, Momma Rosie was a soft-spoken and sweet woman. Amy was imposing, stern, and judgmental to a fault.

After Amy was sent back from Cleveland by her son, King, she settled in her house down the hill from the big house. It was Momma Rosie who looked after her mother-in-law, more out of duty than out of genuine commitment and concern.

When Grandma Amy died in 1936, Momma Rosie had her sons dig a big hole at the base of that huge oak tree. She then threw everything from Amy's house in that hole and made her sons cover it up. I think the only thing that made it out of Amy's house was her picture. She didn't want anything that belonged to her late mother-in-law in her house. That's what Momma Rosie thought of Grandma Amy.

* * * * * * * * * * *

Momma Rosie was such a major influence on us, especially on my sister Christine. Her voice was like a summer breeze, if not a spring rain—pleasant on your ears. She never raised her voice in anger. I can understand why Poppa loved her so much. In fact, it might be more appropriate to say he adored her.

She typically wore a long dress down to her ankles, and often wore a matching bonnet and apron. If she wore dresses even slightly above her ankle, Poppa said, "Rosa, dat skirt is a might short," which would be followed by her standard response, "Sheeeeet. T'ain't nothin' wrong with d'is here skirt, George." That's the closest she ever came to saying a bad word. Momma and Poppa had their twin rocking chairs on the porch and routinely rocked them in unison. Poppa wanted Momma Rosie to stay in the kitchen cooking all day. She always had a pot of pinto beans ready to eat or being prepared. Poppa often said, "Rosa, when you gon' check on dem beans?" "Sheeeeet. Dem beans is okay, George," and would keep fanning herself. That was about as much of a disagreement as you would get out of those two.

Poppa loved his wife, and we all knew it. Once Momma Rosie was ill with the flu or some other ailment that kept her in bed. We loved Momma so much we gladly waited on her hand and foot. We were even ready to get up to empty her slop jar in the middle of the night, but Poppa told us no. "Rosa's my wife. I'm de only one who'll be handlin' her slop jar," he told us. Momma loved and respected Poppa to no end.

In the spring, Momma Rosie would have us go and clean the chicken coop, which meant digging out all the accumulated manure and putting it in her vegetable or flower garden. When you began digging the manure it was manageable, but after the top layer was penetrated, the smell was so strong it burned your eyes. We had to squint as we dug. The ammonia nearly made you pass out, but we loved Momma so much it never dawned on us to tell her we didn't want to clean her chicken coop. Whatever Momma asked us to do, we just did it. Momma Rosie loved flowers. As poor as we were, she kept flowers throughout the house.

She always kept little pieces of peppermint candy in her apron for us. Momma Rosie also loved to crochet. She taught all her daughters (except Wootsie, who wasn't interested in anything like that) and then taught her great-granddaughters, Loretta and Christine. Like Wootsie, I never had much interest in the craft. When she sewed a bonnet and apron, Momma Rosie always made one for Christine, who was the youngest great-granddaughter at that point. Christine always stayed up under her when she was young.

The only time I ever saw Momma Rosie become excitable was once when Doretha's boyfriend, a demon named Cody, was in the house raising hell. Momma walked up behind him and started hitting him on the back of his head with her wicker cane, "You gon' stop dis fuss in Jesus' name! You gon' stop dis fuss in dis house!" She had to have been at least eighty at the time, which meant there was no way she had any strength to hurt him.

I would like to believe my entire life is a testament to Momma Rosie. Everyone knew of her kindness and loving nature.

* * * * * * * * * * *

One of the most important lessons we learned from Momma Rosie was to reject other people's negative views of who we were. She believed it was our job to define ourselves based on our actions and character.

A good example is one incident when Momma Rosie gave us some advice that stuck with us all. It was good in 1959 and it's still good to this day.

When we were children, we caught the school bus in front of Hite's Oil Company and the manager was a White man named Clyde Earles. He was as good a man as you ever wanted to meet in your life, and he later became a reverend. In fact, my brother, sisters, and I decided he was Superman. Right beside the oil company was Fatty Oates' Restaurant. They had a great big "WHITES ONLY" sign on the door and they were very racist. The railroad people ate lunch and dinner there because that's where the trains switched. There were two different rail lines—the Dick and Willie and the Norfolk Western.

One day we got off the bus and Miss Oates had thrown some bottle tops out on the ground between Hite's Oil Company and her store. Because we were kids and loved playing cowboys and Indians, bottle tops were a wonderful thing to have because you could take the cork out of the tops and create a makeshift badge. Dr. Pepper tops were the best because they had numbers (like ten, two, and four) along with a little star on their cap, so we really prized those above the others. We were rummaging through the pile for Dr. Pepper caps so we could all be sheriffs. Lo and behold, Miss Oates came out of the store to run us off calling us "littl' thievin' niggers." She said we were there to steal. We threw the tops down and ran home with her yelling after us. When we got home, we went right to Momma Rosie. Partly in tears, we said, "Miss Oates called us thievin' little niggers." Momma Rosie said, "What she call you dat for?" "Cause we was pickin' up the bottle tops off the ground after she threw 'em out. We wasn't stealin' nothin'. It was just trash."

Momma Rosie said, "Babies, now stop dat d'ere cryin'. You don't pick up trash. You don't pick up *nobody's* trash." That was the end of it. That's as good a lesson today as it was then. Don't pick up trash. I don't mean those bottle tops, but racism and hate—you don't pick it up. You don't need it. Lesson learned.

* * * * * * * * * * * *

I spoke to Christine about this next part because I wanted the family to know more about Momma Rosie and the special relationship they had. There were times when I believed those two were in simpatico with each other. Their relationship was like the one that I had with Grandma Dollie.

When she was young, Christine said she couldn't remember a time when our mother picked us up or hugged us. It made her think sometimes that Doretha didn't love us, especially when she saw the way she was with Loretta. The unconditional motherly love came from Momma Rosie for Christine and from Grandma Dollie for me. In fact, "Momma" (as we referred to her) was the constant reminder of what love felt like throughout our young lives. She never raised her voice to any of us because we were always ready to please her, no matter what she asked. We simply said, "Yes, Momma," and did like she told us. Christine had repeatedly given Doretha back talk, but if Momma Rosie was around, she begrudgingly obeyed her, because she didn't want Momma to see her being disobedient.

Grandma Dollie was like my back-up mother, who also loved me unconditionally, but Dollie was typically away during the week working to support us. She came home on the weekend, but she was still another constant presence in our lives.

In November 1964, the death angel came calling when my sister, Loretta, was tragically killed crossing a train track near Hite's Oil Company. Christine witnessed the entire horrific event. She was so stunned by what she had just seen, she couldn't quite comprehend that she was dead. David had just run across the train track before they had and started screaming after the train struck Loretta. Christine said she just stared at our sister's lifeless body. She said although it will be sixty years in 2024, she still can't erase that image of her lying out near that train track from her head. When I saw her, I knew she had to be in shock because she didn't remember how she got home even though David was walking her back up the hill to the Hollow. He told her about it later. She said she vaguely remembered Doretha screaming at the top of her lungs when she heard the news, but she didn't recall reacting that much.

A few weeks after Loretta's death, Poppa passed away, which was another blow to our family. When Poppa died, Momma Rosie told us kids, as we were grieving, that it wasn't the end of Poppa. We wouldn't see him in this life again, but we would be reunited as she would. Momma said Poppa had been in a lot of pain and his death brought an end to it. When it came to the kids, however, she knew that losing our sister just a few weeks earlier had really been very traumatic for us. Momma kept Christine close to her. Despite her own grief after losing her great-granddaughter and her husband, she sat with Christine every night throughout that period until she fell off to sleep.

That woman's gentle touch on our heads had somehow comforted all of us. She became saintly in all our eyes. When we were growing up and Momma Rosie was away at dinner time, Christine would refuse to eat until she came back home. She was always careful not to be away too long, because she knew Chrissy wouldn't have eaten with her being away.

As if having these back-to-back deaths weren't enough trauma for us, our adolescent world was rocked in 1968 when our beloved Momma Rosie passed away. When Poppa and Loretta died, Christine and I were inconsolable, but when Momma Rosie died, we felt as if our world was about to come to an end.

The year before Momma's death, Uncle Sunny Boy, Doretha's younger brother, passed away suddenly. It was as if part of Momma's soul had left when he died, because she had loved that grandson so much. He had been the apple of her eye. We were never envious of Uncle Sunny Boy because there was more than enough of Momma Rosie to go around. Besides, he made her laugh and was *totally* devoted to her. They had a connection that was also hard to explain, but the two of them understood each other.

After his death, however, Momma would just sit in her rocking chair on the porch and sway back and forth, mourning for her departed Sunny Boy. Sometimes Momma just hummed a church tune as if she was in another world.

Grandma Dollie didn't take her son's death well either. She just shut the entire world out and drank herself into oblivion. I can't even begin to describe how difficult it was for her to lose her son, even though he was an adult. I had never known of a mother losing a child up to that point apart from Doretha losing Loretta. That was so traumatic for her, she had to be taken away for a while.

All of us tried to help Momma deal with Uncle Sunny's death by being extra solicitous to her. We'd ask, "Can I get anything for you, Momma?" Sometimes she would shake her head no to acknowledge us. And other times, it was like she never heard us say a word and just kept rocking back and forth in that chair.

She was in her mid-eighties at the time, but none of us were ready for her to leave. When Doretha was distant toward Christine or me when we were children, it was Momma or Grandma Dollie who stepped in to mother us. Momma Rosie never had to spank me, or be stern with me, because all of the girls wanted to be like her so much.

Momma Rosie departed in spring 1968. Her health just seemed to decline during that final year of her life. A few people believed she died of a broken heart after losing Uncle Sunny Boy. Grandma Dollie and Wootsie took her to Martinsville General Hospital, but she was turned away with the explanation that there was little that could be done for her. They brought her back home, and she lasted just over a week after that.

Grandma Dollie and Wootsie contacted their brother, Uncle Ramey, and their sisters, Aunt Ginny Mae in Bluefield, West Virginia, and Aunt Emily in Roanoke. They all made it back to the Hollow as Momma Rosie was near her end. She died peacefully with her daughters and a few granddaughters sitting around her quilting, and keeping up small talk. Although she was weak, she was able to be propped up in bed and participate a little. In the late afternoon of April 3, Momma Rosie simply lay back in her bed and took her last breath. She was gone as quickly as that. Terry and some other kids were playing under her bed at the time. After Momma passed away, someone got the kids from under her bed and sent them out of the room.

Christine and I were there when she transitioned, but I just assumed she had laid back in the bed to take a nap. One of my aunts felt her wrist for a pulse, and then put an ear on her chest to listen for a heartbeat. She looked around at her sisters and shook her head. The room was totally silent. One by one, each of her daughters, including Wootsie and Grandma Dollie, walked over to Momma Rosie and kissed her goodbye. It was the sweetest scene that I had ever witnessed when I look back on it. A few of them began crying softly, but it was all very contained and reserved. She couldn't have planned a more appropriate and peaceful departure. It suddenly dawned on me at that moment that Momma Rosie had been loved by every single woman in that room. They loved her as much as her great-grandchildren had. I just stood there stunned until Grandma Dollie walked me outside. She said something to me, but I tuned everything out.

The day Momma Rosie died, Christine stopped eating and speaking. A few times, she later told me, she consciously tried to stop breathing. She didn't cry or react in any way. Doretha, Wootsie, and Grandma Dollie tried to get her to eat or at least interact with the other kids, but she refused. She was just numb. Aunt Ginny Mae told them not to force her. She said she just needed time to process what had happened. She somehow understood the depths of my sister's feelings for Momma Rosie. Christine told me that at the time, she was determined to never eat again. The others became alarmed that she would starve herself to death.

Much later, Christine told me that a week or so after her death, Momma Rosie visited her in a dream. In it, she was lying on the porch crying because Momma had died. She heard this soft voice calling her quietly from the road leading to the Hollow, "Chrissy . . . . Chrissy . . . . Chrissy Baby." She stopped crying, looked up and saw Momma Rosie moving up the dirt road. She was wearing a white translucent gown and moving very slowly. It almost seemed as if she was floating. When Christine narrated the dream to me, it was a little eerie, but it captured Momma's voice with incredible accuracy.

"Chrissy, I want chu' to stop dis here cryin' and come wit' me. Come on, right now."

"Momma, everyone said you're dead. If I go with you, won't I die too?"

She nodded her head affirmatively.

"You want me to go with you and die?"

"Well, if you don't wanna' come wit' me, you need to stop dis' here cryin' and eat, child."

"Yes, Momma."

"I'll tell you what. When it's your time to cross over, I'll come back to get you, Baby. I promise."

"Yes, Momma. You promise, Momma?"

She nodded her head, turned, and began moving away. As she moved away, Christine thought for a moment that maybe she should go with her, but she hesitated to call Momma Rosie back, because if she had done so, she would have to die. Christine told me she woke up the next morning with tears in her eyes, hating the fact that she would not see our great-grandmother again in this life. But she remembered what Momma Rosie said, and she firmly believes that when her time comes, our beloved grandmother will fulfill her promise and come back for her.

When Momma Rosie was buried at old Mountain Top Cemetery, the plan was to bury her next to her husband. The funeral people, however, did not have the records on Poppa's exact burial location, so they placed Momma Rosie next to Grandma Amy who had been buried several feet in front of Poppa. They must have thought it was okay to place her there, so that's where they dug the hole. But Momma Rosie would never have approved of such. She did *not* like her stern and severe mother-in-law. She never spoke ill of her, but her dislike of Amy manifested itself when she ordered her sons to dig that hole after Amy's death and threw all the old woman's things in it.

After Momma Rosie died, we all tried to have a better relationship with Doretha. It was a challenge given all that had taken place. Christine had confronted her more than once and accused her of not loving her children. She was also quick to talk back to her. Christine said it wasn't until after she got saved and joined the church that she began softening her heart toward her. I came to understand that Momma Rosie had not judged her, her mother-in-law Amy, or her daughter Dollie for having out-of-wedlock children. Momma had a child out of wedlock herself, and therefore refused to judge her mother-in-law, her daughter, or her granddaughter for having done the same. We never knew the circumstances. It was another one of those subjects that wasn't spoken of. Christine said she had not intended to go down that road.

Christine and the other kids *had* to learn to love Doretha after Momma left, but Christine made a serious vow at fifteen-years old. She determined that she would not be the same kind of mother to her children that Doretha had been to us. She would also not have children out of wedlock and count-less boyfriends. Lastly, she said her children would receive the kind of love that Momma Rosie and Grandma Dollie had given us. That's how she began the process of loving Doretha, but it wasn't without its challenges. We know Momma Rosie wouldn't have had it any other way.

When Christine's oldest daughter, Melinda, was born, she expected Doretha to help her out the way a daughter might expect a mother to assist with her new grandbaby. But she was strangely distant, if not standoffish. When Melinda was about two years old, Christine noticed something about her.

She reminded her of someone but couldn't figure out who it was. It then occurred to her that the little girl was the spitting image of our sister Loretta. She had her complexion, her hairline, her body shape, and her legs. Christine asked our mother about it.

"Doretha, do you think Melinda favors Loretta?"

"She looks just like her. I saw the resemblance right after she was born. It scared me so, I was afraid to be around her."

"Why is that, Doretha?"

"She reminded me so much of Loretta, it was painful for me to see Melinda."

None of us had any idea that this had been going on in Doretha's mind. When I thought about it, Doretha was one of the few people who would have known what Loretta looked like as a newborn. That brief exchange between Doretha and Christine seemed to have freed her somehow. Because after that, it was as if the sun rose and set on Melinda's head. She could do no wrong as far as Doretha was concerned.

When Melinda was about five or six, she saw a picture of Loretta on the mantle. In the picture, Loretta was about five or six and Christine, David, and I were also in the photograph. She asked Christine,

"Momma, when did you take this picture of me? And who are these other children?"

"No, sweetheart, that's not you. That's your Aunt Loretta who died before you were born. And that's Aunt Naomi, Uncle David, and me."

Although Christine told me about this episode, she never told Doretha about Melinda's observation. I agreed with that. That would have been too much for our mother to handle. Doretha never got over Loretta's death. But somehow having Melinda near made her feel like Loretta wasn't completely gone and she had her daughter back, being raised by Christine.

Doretha bought Melinda's first saxophone, and when she was crowned Miss Virginia Union, she and Christine stayed up all night long to make her gown. They were up until 6:00 AM working on that dress. Doretha *had* to put the finishing touches on it. When she graduated from the Shenandoah Conservatory, Christine was away and couldn't attend the commencement. Doretha was right there in her place. She was in her element when it came to her grandchildren.

5

Dollie Mariah Finney

*A*fter Great-Great-Grandma Amy, Poppa, and Momma Rosie passed away, Grandma Dollie became our famiy's sometimes-reluctant matriarch. She was one of the most pivotal figures in our family, and a tragic figure in certain ways. Dollie Mariah Finney (aka Dollie Slaughter, Dollie Walker, and "Grandma Dollie") was born in Horse Pasture, Virginia in 1911. It is because of Dollie that the Koehler Hollow legacy has been preserved. She became the unofficial keeper of family records and the principal custodian of her grandmother Amy's legacy. Grandma Amy realized that Dollie had a higher-than-average intelligence as well as a remarkable memory.

Her first of two children was Doretha Lee Finney, born in 1927. Doretha was conceived out of wedlock with Dollie's second cousin, Jesse Ben Hairston when she was fifteen and Jesse Ben was nineteen. Because second cousins having sexual relations was considered taboo (the unofficial line was drawn at third cousin), a scandal resulted. Jesse Ben was sent away, but Dollie had to face the shame of an out-of-wedlock pregnancy with her second cousin. Three years later, she had another child out of wedlock, James Alfred Finney, better known as Uncle "Sunny Boy," in March 1930. There are no details as to who his father was. Dollie never volunteered that information, and it just wasn't spoken of. We believed Poppa and Momma Rosie may have known more about the situation, but neither of them ever spoke of it.

Grandma Dollie did not lack for suitors. On December 16, 1933, she married a man named Ben Slaughter who had once pitched in the Negro Baseball League. Ben was said to have gotten into an argument with another man who called him a "son of a whore" or some other rude name. Ben picked up a rock and threw it at the man so hard that he split his skull open and killed him. Ben was arrested and convicted of manslaughter and served time in prison for the man's death.

In 1937, Grandma Dollie remarried, this time to a man named Leonard Walker. The problem was she never divorced Ben Slaughter. Some years after Ben was released from prison, he wanted to get back with Dollie, but she wasn't interested. Ben was so angry he reported his wife to the authorities saying she had "remarried" without divorcing him. Grandma Dollie was prosecuted and sent to prison for bigamy for about three months. Eventually, Leonard Walker left for some unknown reason and never returned. Grandma Dollie remained single the rest of her life.

I met Ben Slaughter when I was about twelve. He came to visit Grandma Dollie at the Hollow. They were both in their fifties then. The visit was very cordial, and they were quite polite to each other. That was the only time I remember seeing him. It was only after he left that Grandma said they had been married years earlier. She said it in a very matter-of-fact manner, but instinctively I knew not to ask any other questions about Mr. Slaughter. She never said any more on the subject.

It would be an understatement to say that Grandma Dollie was a very bright woman. She could have been a teacher, if not a lawyer, with her intelligence. She had a memory like an elephant. Even with only a seventh-grade education, she could quote Shakespeare and recite poetry *beautifully*. When I studied Shakespeare in high school, I had an advantage, because I had heard Grandma Dollie recite several of those monologues. I knew Hamlet's famous soliloquy "To be or not to be . . ." long before I studied the play in high school, because Grandma Dollie had recited it to me. She made me love poetry. I can recite well today because of her.

It's a shame Poppa didn't have the money to send Grandma Dollie to the Presbyterian school in Martinsville, where she could have easily flourished. No doubt she would have been a superb teacher.

Like so many Black women, regardless of their potential for success, Dollie worked as a domestic. The White women she worked for picked her up on Sunday afternoon and took her from the family with her shopping bag that held her clothes for the week. She was returned to the Hollow on Friday afternoon.

Dollie's work was in such demand that she could pick and choose her employers. Sometimes she'd work for a woman and then stop either because she didn't like the family or the job was complete. She worked for so many women sometimes it seemed like a bidding process. Once Dollie took a job because the woman's foot was the same size as mine and Dollie made that a part of her negotiation—that is, procuring shoes (although used) for me.

When Grandma Dollie came back on Fridays, so did her sister, Wootsie, who also worked as a domestic. The average pay was about fifteen dollars a week, but a good domestic worker could get as much as eighteen dollars. A seasoned worker like Grandma Dollie, however, could get even more because there was such a high demand for her services.

For a good deal of the twentieth century, Henry County was a bootlegging county. It was only surpassed in production in Virginia by Franklin County. There were tons of bootleggers, and drinking was the norm. Aunt Wootsie loved to drink. She enjoyed the taste of liquor, and the alcohol was a release for her to raise a little hell. Grandma Dollie, on the other hand, drank to temper the effects of her chronic asthma. Most likely it also helped her deal with depression. She said more than once that she hated the taste of liquor, yet she drank as a way of self-medicating.

Whenever Wootsie and Grandma Dollie came home for the weekend, Wootsie would pour herself a teacup of bootleg liquor. Sometimes she went to Mr. Franks and brought back a pint of bootleg. David and I would put water in her liquor to slow down her high. Wootsie had a high tolerance for alcohol. She could drink all night and you could barely tell she was high. Grandma Dollie was the opposite. A few sips seemed to do her in.

As a child, I worried about Grandma Dollie leaving the house walking down the hill to her place after drinking, so I would leave my brothers and sisters at night and follow her. She'd get unsteady after a few drinks. I was no more than ten, yet I felt she needed me to help her make it to her house safely. I never uttered a word, and neither would she, but she knew I was following her. I usually shed tears the whole way down, but I felt protective of her.

When we made it inside her place, I'd crawl up in the bed with her and she would lie there with me for a while until I went to sleep and then get back up. I believe she had insomnia because she just couldn't stay asleep all night. Sometimes when I didn't fall to sleep right away, I would lie beside her and just look at her.

She'd say, "Close your eyes, 'cause I can see you." It would be pitch black in that room. I'd whisper back to her,

"Grannie, you can't see my eyes."

"Yes, I can. Close those eyes, gal." That was our routine.

Grandma Dollie was very calm and quiet just like her mother, Momma Rosie. She rarely screamed and was extremely patient above all. She was a sweet, but wounded soul.

Grandma Dollie could quote Paul Lawrence Dunbar's dialectical poems like "In the Morning," but had an affinity for his love poetry. Her favorite Dunbar poem was "Invitation to Love:"

> *"Come when the nights are bright with stars*
> *Or come when the moon is mellow;*
> *Come when the sun his golden bars*
> *Drops on the hay field yellow . . . ."*

She could recite lengthy poems of Langston Hughes, Shakespeare, and many others. Dollie was that gifted, but there was no opportunity for her to be anything but a domestic. That, along with her failed marriages and a daughter who didn't love her or even like her that much, just haunted grandmother. Dollie didn't see many wins in her life. It's not that she lacked love, because I adored her. And her son, Uncle Sunny Boy, was totally devoted to his mother, and loved her unconditionally.

While Doretha had a strained relationship with Grandma Dollie, my relationship with her was the very opposite. I worshipped the woman. I loved her so much because she made me feel as if I was the most special child in the world. She was more like a momma to me than a grandma. She took me to Norfolk with her within a few months of my birth, so I bonded with Grandma Dollie more than I did with Doretha. Dollie was the world to me. I followed her everywhere. She often quoted the Robert Louis Stevenson poem:

"I have a little shadow that
goes in and out with me,
and what can be the use of him
is more than I can see . . ."

I walked behind her everywhere she went. The people she worked for sometimes allowed her to bring me. Grandma Dollie had another saying which I believe came from a narrative from the time of enslavement,

"Grannie's baby black and sweet
just like candy that you eat . . ."

I said, "Grannie, what kind of candy am I?" "You're a Baby Ruth, because you are full of nuts." Even today you will find a Baby Ruth chocolate bar in my freezer or somewhere in my house in her memory.

She always hummed when she was in the kitchen, and it was typically a religious tune. Grandma Dollie was also one of the most patient persons you ever met, but she was also hurt. You could see the hurt she suffered, because of the circumstances surrounding Doretha's birth. She felt ashamed, and you could see it in her eyes. Even I could see it as a young girl. There were times I just wanted to tell her to let go of those feelings, but they were too deep for anyone to reach. She believed she was destined to do much better in life, and she had let everyone down—herself most of all.

I think Poppa and Momma Rosie were disappointed with Dollie because of the out-of-wedlock children. After all, Poppa was an AME minister and an elder of the church. Maybe Poppa took some of the blame for Dollie's fall because she had qualified to attend the regional high school academically, but he just didn't have the money to send her. If there was any disappointment with his daughter, it was unspoken. I never heard Poppa say a mean thing to or about Dollie and I never heard a bad word exchanged between them.

Aunt Wootsie, on the other hand, as Poppa and Momma Rosie's youngest child, was a natural born hellraiser. She was defiant just for the sake of being defiant. She'd get drunk and lay Poppa out about being in her business and telling her what to do. "So what if I drink? Hell, what else is there to do here? I'm supposed to go to hell 'cause I'm drinkin'?" At a point, Wootsie opened a bootleg joint in Dollie's house since she was away during the week. When Poppa told her not to do it, Wootsie defiantly said, "Yes, I am," and did so.

Grandma Dollie, on the other hand, was the dutiful daughter. She cooked for her parents and when Poppa got a high blood pressure diagnosis, she had him on a special diet. She cared for both her parents, but I can't say they were close. I just didn't see the same love and affection that Dollie displayed toward me and Uncle Sunny Boy for Poppa and Momma Rosie. She impressed on me that she was more of a servant than a daughter.

Doretha claimed Grandma Dollie never showed her any love and said she thought her mother was distant. According to her, she thought for a long time that Wootsie was her mother which was most certainly an exaggeration at best. She said it was Wootsie who gave her hugs and kisses, and Dollie didn't care about her. The relationship between Doretha and Grandma Dollie was tense and often toxic throughout both their lives. More than once, Doretha accused Grandma Dollie of eating peppers during her pregnancy to abort her. She said Grandma Dollie didn't want to have her because of her age. Doretha triumphantly continued, "I still made it here!" Of course, none of those things were true, but that didn't stop her from making such hateful statements.

Being my grandmother's little girl, I found most of the negative things Doretha said about Dollie hard to believe. Grandma Dollie was nothing but loving to me, and she had a very strong mother/son relationship with Uncle Sunny Boy. Because Dollie was ostracized and looked down upon because she had an out-of-wedlock child, Doretha felt she had a foundation for her resentment. However, Grandma Dollie was only nineteen when she had Uncle Sunny Boy which means she wasn't much older when she had Doretha and there wasn't even the hint of negativity between those two. I believe Doretha just got it into her head (or had it fed to her by someone like Aunt Alice, which is a later story), that her mother didn't love her.

Grandma Dollie had started working outside the home at thirteen. Because she had a child to support when she was sixteen years old, she had to make a living. Doretha had Momma Rosie, Wootsie, and Aunt Alice (although she turned out to be a negative influence), who doted on her. Doretha was the first granddaughter to be born and grow up in the Hollow and certainly got a lot of attention. When I was born, I was Dollie's first granddaughter. She doted on me the way she hadn't doted on her daughter. I'm sorry to say that Doretha and Grandma Dollie went to their respective graves with those issues unresolved.

* * * * * * * * * * *

I started college in 1970 and am a proud alumna of Virginia Union University in Richmond. I started at nineteen instead of eighteen because I had to repeat the sixth grade, due to contracting pneumonia and missing nearly two months of school. Although Poppa tutored me, and I passed all the required exams, there was a rule that a student could miss no more than a certain number of days from school. If the limit was passed, the student was required to be held back a year. That repeated year turned out to be the best thing that could have happened to me, although I initially thought I was a failure. Before that, I was severely bullied. Kids pulled my hair and called me names daily. The anonymity of the class that came afterward was like a fresh start.

My Virginia Union experience opened a new world for me in so many ways. The inconspicuousness of living in a large city like Richmond was exhilarating, not to mention the dormitory and campus atmosphere. For the first time in my life, I felt totally liberated. There were no small-town eyes looking over my shoulders or saying things like, "Ain't you so and so's chap?" The library, the books—it could all be overwhelming but in a positive way.

In what was to have been my sophomore year, however, I didn't have enough money to return. I had an academic scholarship which paid my tuition, but I didn't have enough to pay for my room and board, as well as my books. So, at twenty years old, I had to stay home and get a job. On that job, Grandma Dollie's wisdom kept me safe in a rough situation.

I managed to get work at American Furniture in the rough end. That was the section that cuts raw timber into slats big enough to make furniture like dressers or tables. I tailed a rider saw which had a double blade. If you were making a 36-inch board, for example, you would open thirty-six inches to have the two blades cut off the wood at the same time. If you needed a shorter board, you adjusted the blades accordingly. They wouldn't give us gloves or goggles which meant you got splinters in your hands and face. If you forgot and wiped your face, you would scratch yourself. They only passed out protective hand- and eyewear when they were facing an OSHA inspection.

I called the man in charge of the rider saw "Spits" because he loved to spit right at your shoes. In fact, he'd spit directly on your shoes if you didn't watch out. He was a tall, slender, White man of about forty-five with salt-and-pepper hair. He was also a real hardcore racist. He ran the saw as fast as he could so I couldn't get the lumber off the pulley without a few of the slabs spilling over on the floor or hitting me. He would just keep them coming. Spits refused to slow it down to a pace more manageable for me to pick up the boards and set them on the little wagon-like buggy. I had to pack this buggy with cut wood up to eye level before I had to push it off to another area for further processing.

Spits prided himself for running the saw faster than I could keep up with it. The lumber would back up and hit me on my shins and a few times on my knees, which didn't help my legs. He would only stop before the machine jammed or broke down from going too fast. And he would spit at me on the ground as a sign of his disapproval of a woman doing this kind of work.

We also had a White foreman who was a piece of work. Based on his appearance, you would have thought he was a sweet guy. He was a tall, nicely built White man with snow white hair and a winning smile that he didn't hesitate to greet you with. He wore a clean, neatly pressed khaki uniform every day. But behind that appearance he was a nasty, filthy man.

Every day that man would reach in his pocket on the side of his belt and pull his measuring ruler out to six or eight inches to indicate the length of his penis. He'd then say, "I'm gon' get you behind that stack of wood, Buckwheat, and you know what's comin' next," waving that measuring stick at me. Yep, that was my name in 1971, "Buckwheat." That man terrified me. The company cut the lights out in the furniture factory at twelve noon for lunch and they didn't come back on until one o'clock. The work was so hard you needed an hour just to recover and the break prevented the machines from over-heating; at least that's what we were told. But before the lights came back on, I had to walk through the darkened factory to be back at my workstation by 1:00 PM on the dot. Otherwise, I would be docked for being late. When I clocked back in after lunch the factory floor was still dark. That foreman would sometimes jump out of the dark and say, "Hey Buckwheat! I got'cha now!" He had me on pins and needles.

One day, that man had taunted me so much that when I got home, I was sitting out in front of the house as nervous as a cat. Tears were streaming down my face when Grandma Dollie saw me and knew something was wrong.

"Gal, what's ailin' you?"

"Nothin'."

"Gal, somethin' ain't right wit' you. What is it?" I broke down crying at that point. She let me get it out of my system.

I then told her what that old evil foreman had said and how he'd pull out his ruler and threaten to rape me. I was afraid to tell Pokechop, Doretha's second husband, because he would have just gone there and gut-shot the foreman dead. If that had happened, I would have been stuck at Koehler Hollow and would never have gotten back to college. Grandma Dollie said, "Gal, I want you to know somethin'. I don' worked in White folk's kitchens all my life, servin' tables and the like, and I'm a tell you right now: ain't no man laid his hands on me savin' I wanted him to. You take care of yo' business and *stop* this cryin'." She then looked me directly in the eyes and said, "Sweet girl, you remember, a coward dies a thousand deaths, a brave man oh but once." Grandma Dollie, who only went to the seventh grade, had just quoted Shakespeare's *Julius Caesar* to me.

Somehow, her comments lifted a weight off my shoulders. Grandma didn't tell me what to do, as strange as it may seem. She didn't have to. But I understood she meant that I needed to cut that son of a bitch if he threatened me again. So, I went to town the very next day and bought me a switchblade knife at Robbie's Army Surplus Outlet. I oiled that knife so it would just pop out with the slightest flip of my wrist. I sharpened the blade so much that I could cut off the little hair I had on my legs.

I went back to work with that switchblade in my pocket and an inner vow that I was going to take care of my business. Monday came and the man did nothing. Tuesday, nothing happened; Wednesday, the same. My nerves started unwinding, and I became a little less nervous. Before that, I was as jittery as a cat in a room full of rocking chairs. I think that foreman noticed something different about me and left me alone. Thursday came and went, and nothing happened. Friday arrived. I was walking through the factory in the dark, and that foreman was the last thing on my mind. I put my card in the machine, punched back in, and walked past a stack of timber. Sure enough, that son of a bitch jumped out and shouted, "I got you now, Buckwheat!" Almost reflexively, I reached in my pocket, flipped out that knife, crouched down low and said, "Come on! I'm a cut 'chu every way but loose! Just come on, come on!"

Lo and behold he backed up and said, "Wooo, Suzy-Q. I ain't mean nothin' by it." I got a promotion from "Buckwheat" to "Suzy-Q" in the matter of a few seconds when he realized I was as serious as a heart attack. It made me so mad, I wanted to cut him on general principle. He had terrorized me for months and now all of a sudden here, he was punkin' down. On top of that, thereafter, I was called "Suzy-Q." So, the moral of this story is what my Grandma Dollie told me on those steps. "Take care of your business, and a coward dies a thousand deaths."

Grandma Dollie's wisdom appeared to be infinite. All I needed to do was go to her. Were it not for the prevailing customs of the period and being in the South, she might have been a lawyer, if not a judge. I recognized her brilliance when I was young. At that time, I thought she could do anything. Her favorite expression when she knew someone was lying was, "That's your tale, I'll sit on mine." That was the closest she came to calling someone a liar.

6

Doretha and Jesse Ben

My mother's given name was Doretha Lee Finney. She was born at the main house in Koehler Hollow in 1927. Her grandmother, the once-enslaved Amy, delivered her into the world. Grandma Dollie named her daughter Doretha but did not give her a middle name. There was one other Black family in Koehler, the Goins. Their matriarch, Miss Alice, proudly traced her family's lineage back to General Robert E. Lee. She suggested to Grandma Dollie that mother have the middle name "Lee." So, this little Black girl born in 1927 was given the middle name "Lee" after the Confederate Civil War general.

I remember Miss Alice telling us that Robert E. Lee was her great-grandfather. She sang this song, "Waiting on the Robert E. Lee," which she also played on the mandolin. I, in turn, was also given the middle name "Lee" after Doretha. "Naomi Lee" turned out to be the irony of ironies. The president of the

Martinsville chapter of the NAACP bears the middle name of Robert E. Lee. Only in Virginia would you find this.

Doretha was a very pretty woman. In fact, when I was a child, I thought she was the color of sunshine. She had beautiful bronze skin with a yellow glow about her with long, wavy shoulder-length hair. She was gorgeous as a young woman. As a baby girl, Aunt Wootsie doted on her. In a word, Doretha was spoiled by Wootsie and Dollie's brothers and sisters. So all my life I was raised by a spoiled person.

My mother loved to tell me about her childhood, which was comical. She was never one to back down from a fight and often instigated them. She could also carry a mean grudge. When she was about eight years old, Momma Rosie had left to do ironing for a White couple just outside of Koehler. Momma Rosie told Doretha to stay off her sewing machine because she didn't know what she was doing. Just as soon as Momma Rosie left, Doretha decided that she was going to do some sewing. She was sewing pretty well on several things at first, but around noon, she broke the needle. Now this was not an electric machine, but a treadle model where you had to use your foot to work the wheel. Scared after she had broken that needle, Doretha asked their neighbor, Miss Alice, if she had a replacement needle, but she didn't have one. Doretha kept going around to other houses asking for a needle. She went to another neighbor, Miss Wright, who was White. As it turned out Miss Wright had a spare needle. Doretha begged her to loan it to her and not to tell Momma Rosie because she had told her not to get on the machine. Doretha promised Miss Wright she would replace the needle the following day.

Doretha skipped back home, put the replacement needle back in the machine, and put everything back as it was supposed to be. Somehow, she made up her mind that she was going to get to the store to get Miss Wright's needle back, even if she had to steal it. Later, that day, as Momma Rosie was coming home, she passed by the Wrights' house. Miss Wright made it a point to come out to tell Momma Rosie her granddaughter had come by earlier to borrow a needle. Momma Rosie thanked Miss Wright, but before she got home she went to the hedges and got herself a good switch. Doretha saw her picking out the switches before she came into the house but could not imagine they were for her. No sooner did Momma Rosie get in the house, but she grabbed Doretha by the arm and gave her a good switching. As she was being switched, Momma Rosie told Doretha, "I tol' ya not ta mess wit' dat machine." Mother knew immediately Miss Wright had told Momma Rosie about the broken needle and was infuriated after her beating. She had promised Miss Wright that she would get her needle back to her, but in her eight-year-old mind, she had been betrayed.

About two weeks later, early in the morning, Doretha got up before everyone. She also got her brother Sunny Boy up and they left the house. The two of them went down the road to the Wrights' house. They sneaked in the back and Doretha went inside the Wrights' chicken coop. She set aside some eggs that she wanted. She then put the other eggs in a row, took a rock, and smashed them up. Uncle Sunny Boy said nervously, "Dody why'd you do that?" Doretha said, "I paid her back for tellin' on me." She gathered her eggs and skipped back home with Uncle Sunny Boy following her, feeling guilty even though he had done nothing. That was the mentality of my mother at eight years old. As it turned out, it was only a forecast of what was coming.

* * * * * * * * * * *

When she was young, Doretha was a bright sunny child. She was happy, goofy, and loved to laugh and dance. She also sucked her two middle fingers which was a habit that she developed in childhood and carried into her adult life. She'd come in from work at Jobbers Pants Factory, eat her dinner, spank whomever had misbehaved, and go to bed. Sometimes our dog at the time, King Boy, would prevent her from spanking us by nipping at her. We thought it was an effective strategy for King Boy to be around when we were punished. Doretha would then crawl up on the bed and put those two middle fingers in her mouth and go to sleep. For some reason she stopped that habit after Loretta was killed. She was more like a big sister than a mother—a big sister who wasn't quite right.

Doretha was never an affectionate woman. I never knew her to kiss and hug on anybody. When she combed our hair, it was pure hell. She had three daughters, which meant she had three heads to do, and it was rough—pure agony. My hair hung below my shoulders, but it was also coarse. She'd hit the top of my head with that comb and raked down like she was angry. I cried throughout the process because I was tender-headed. When I went to college, I cut my hair off and wore an afro.

Despite her faults, Doretha encouraged her children. She never said we couldn't do anything. She always encouraged our dreams and aspirations. That was probably her best virtue. If you told her you were going to the moon, she'd say, "Really? How are you gon' to do that? You know you have to study hard to get there." I have to say that was the most positive thing that I got from being raised by Doretha—she had total belief in her children and encouraged us to do anything we set our minds to. She didn't think kids should be told no when it came to their dreams. I admired that about her.

Of her children, I was the only one who did not routinely call her "Doretha." She wanted us to call her by her first name, because she felt she looked too young to be anyone's mother. But I sometimes insisted on calling her "Mother," or "Mama," instead of Doretha. I didn't care if she didn't like it. It just didn't strike me as appropriate to call her by her first name when all of the kids from school called their parents "Mama," "Daddy," or some variation. She was a different kind of person for that time. She had also called her mother "Dollie."

When she met Jesse Ben Hodge, Doretha said he was one of the prettiest "niggas" she had ever seen in her life. He was tall and thin just like her grandfather, George Finney. She met Jesse Ben after a relationship she had with a boy named

Alfred. He had been Doretha's first love, but when they went to see her mother for approval to court, Grandma Dollie didn't say yea or nay to the marriage. The three of them just sat and Dollie didn't offer an opinion. Doretha couldn't figure out how to tell Dollie that she wanted to marry Alfred. Instead of going to Poppa and Momma Rosie for their blessing, Doretha and Alfred didn't do anything. The young man simply gave up and joined the Navy. I think she blamed losing Alfred on Grandma Dollie.

In any case, Doretha met Jesse Ben at a party after World War II in the late 1940s. She said he wore the shiniest shoes along with a beautiful suit. She later found out that Jesse Ben had been put up to talking to her on a dare from some of his buddies. They thought he wasn't brave enough to go over and speak to that pretty gal on a bet. That's how Jesse Ben came into Doretha's life.

Originally from Axton, Virginia, Jesse Ben Hodge was full of aspirations of greatness, but did not possess the work ethic to fulfill these dreams. Doretha liked him because he was very articulate and used big words. He didn't speak like the other men whom she had encountered. Doretha often swore I was just like him. She said he looked up words in the dictionary that he could use in conversations and was always interested in expanding his vocabulary. Even so, Jesse Ben Hodge had the same seventh-grade education as most African Americans in the region of that era. None of that stopped Doretha from falling in love with him.

He proposed marriage to Doretha and told her that if she said no he would stand out on the track and let the train run him down. I think Mother also had marriage fever, because she was twenty-three at the time and many girls her age were already married. Being as pretty as she was, I think Doretha felt the social pressure of tying the knot. She should have listened carefully to Jesse Ben's entreaties because if a man tells you he will kill himself if you don't marry him, it's likely you are not his first choice.

They married in 1949. He gave her a set of silverware as a wedding present. Jesse Ben worked at Martinsville's Novelty Furniture Factory, and they lived in Grandma Amy's cottage in the Hollow.

Jesse Ben had great taste when it came to furniture and wanted to be a big-time dresser. So even though he worked regularly, he'd spend his money on clothes. He seems not to have realized that he had kids to feed within a few years of marriage. That was a woman's job as far as he was concerned. What Jesse Ben didn't spend on clothes, he'd use to gamble. He was supposedly good at it, but that didn't put bread on the table either. Before he finally left the area, Jesse Ben ran up a sizable tab at a suit store in Martinsville and left Doretha to pay the bill.

Around 2005, I received a call from a social worker who was affiliated with a hospice facility in Cleveland, Ohio. The woman told me that Jesse Ben Hodge was at the facility and had listed me as his next of kin. I only recalled meeting him once as an adult, years before when his mother, Grandma Vergie, died. Of course, he came back home for her funeral. He came up to me and asked if I knew who he was. I knew, of course. He said I had grown to resemble his mother, but he was one of the few who saw that resemblance. We had a cordial enough conversation, and I gave him a business card with my cell and home number on the back. He held onto that card for years and that's how the hospice facility knew how to reach me.

After they contacted me, I called Jesse Ben's sister, Aunt Virginia, and explained that her brother was dying. She promptly asked me what I was going to do. Of course, I understood the meaning of the question and knew I couldn't expect much from that side of the family.

I bought Jesse Ben a ticket to fly home and explained to the airline that he was unable to walk. The airline flew him into Greensboro and Doretha and I drove down to pick him up. He was in a wheelchair when we met him and looked quite emaciated from when I had last seen him.

On the drive back to Martinsville, Jesse Ben bragged about the money he had made and the fancy cars he had driven. I'm sure it was some kind of defense mechanism to deflect from his current situation. I didn't really pay a lot of attention to him until he said something about the year 1970. I had a brief flashback to that year—Grandma Dollie had sent me a $3 money order and Doretha had struggled to send me a $10 monthly money order. Here was Jesse Ben Hodge, my birth father, being driven in my car en route to my house in the suburbs telling

me what money he made and what kind of fancy cars he had
driven. I thought to myself, "You ain't worth a good damn!
Here you are headed to my house telling me how affluent you
were at a time when I was struggling my ass off trying to make
it through school. I don't know why I went to get you. God
must have had a reason to put you back in my life." It made me
angry to just sit and listen to him brag.

After we got settled back home, I told Doretha about my
feelings. "Can you believe him telling us about how much he
made when I was dirt poor in college?" Mother's response to
my statement was:

"The best thing that nigga ever done was to leave us.
'Cause if he hadn't, I'da killed him."

"What! Really!?"

"Yeah, that's the truth. If he hadn't left, I would'a killed
him, and you and your brother wouldn't have had a mother or
a father in your lives, 'cause I would'a been in jail for murder."

Doretha wasn't just blowing smoke when she said it was
likely that she would have killed Jesse Ben. She came close
to doing it back in the 1950s. When I told the story about
Grandma Amy's house burning down, there was more to it
than I initially indicated. It was while Doretha was expecting
me. Jesse Ben had been out all evening and left a very pregnant
Doretha back home with a newborn, son. When he got back to
the Hollow, Doretha asked him about some comic books he
was supposed to bring her. When he told her he didn't have
them, they got into a huge argument—over comic books, if you

can imagine that. Jesse Ben eventually slapped Doretha's face for being insolent, thinking that would be the end of the matter. He went about his business and started undressing to go to bed. Doretha, never a wilting violet, got the shotgun from over the front door. When Jesse Ben saw Doretha with the shotgun, he took off, half-dressed, out the door. Doretha, however, had a bead on him and was ready to shoot. Fortunately, Uncle Sunny Boy, who was about twenty-three at the time, must have heard Doretha and Jesse Ben arguing and went over to Grandma Amy's cottage to investigate. He happened to arrive just as Doretha was about to pull the trigger of the shotgun. Reflexively, Uncle Sunny pushed the shotgun barrel up, and the bullet went into the air and missed Jesse Ben, who kept running.

Unfortunately, Jesse Ben Hodge grew up in a household where it was standard for a man to smack a woman around. He was not alone in that behavior. But Grandma Dollie had warned Doretha and all her girls about accepting any domestic violence from any man they were involved with. I remember her quote on the subject quite well:

> "You don't let no man beat on you, honey. As women, that first beatin' is on him. The second one is on *you*. You don't tolerate it, child. A pot of hot sugar water works wonders if you ain't got no gun. Let that fool go off to bed and make him think he's safe. Then you boil you a pot full of sugar water and let him get good

an' sleep. Then you *throw* it on him with all the
force your arms will allow, and then you run.
Don't even wait for 'em to holla. Be sure your
bag is packed. And don't you never go back
to him after that, or you will really be stupid."

Doretha had a *shotgun* in the house, so she didn't have to
boil any sugar water for Jesse Ben. Besides, there was nowhere
for her to run. She and Jesse Ben were living in her grandmother's house.

However, Jesse Ben got the final word, according to Doretha.
He came back sometime later and burned Grandma Amy's
house down to the ground to get even with his wife. No one
could ever prove it, but he was seen in the area prior to the start
of the fire and he never denied that he was responsible. No one
was in the house at the time, but everything was lost. Doretha
and Jesse Ben never really reconciled properly after that, but
they continued having marital relations.

Doretha and I sat in silence for a few minutes after she told
me that story. I had to reconsider my anger. She finally broke
her silence by saying, "It didn't kill you. His runnin' off made
you into the woman you are." It was a struggle, but there was
a reason Jesse Ben was with me at the end of his life. He was
there to bring me over the top of the hate and resentment I
had held on to for so long. During those three weeks he was in
my life to die, I came to realize I had to forgive him and make
peace with that entire episode, even though he had been an ass

in his day. So, when I buried him, I buried those bitter feelings at the same time.

My brother David didn't have the same negative feelings. I felt those feelings every time someone who knew Jesse Ben Hodge would say to me, "You look just like your daddy." Every time I met a Hodge they threw that comment in my face. It felt like a dagger in my heart, because I looked like someone who didn't give a good damn about me. Yet here I was helping him to transition out of this world.

The local hospice people came to my house to help him. Jesse Ben became so disoriented after about a week with me that he attempted to drive one of my cars, even without keys to do so. I'm not sorry I helped him out in the end. I believe it was more for me than him anyway. I carried some serious feelings about all of that, as I said. Having Jesse Ben in my home for that brief period helped me to process those issues before he passed away. These are not easy things to say.

7

Wootsie (1916–1985)

*A*my Gertrude Finney, better known as "Wootsie" to those who knew her well, was our most colorful aunt. She was every bit as important to our family and how we grew up as Momma Rosie, Poppa, and Grandma Dollie. Aunt Wootsie was a tomboy when she was young. Poppa officially named his youngest daughter after his mother. I don't think Wootsie really liked her given name, because I never knew anyone who called her anything but "Wootsie." Even Momma Rosie and Poppa called her by that name. She loved to fish, shoot guns, and wear pants. Wootsie also loved to whistle—among her habits that Poppa most disliked. He felt it was unbecoming and unlady-like. He often quoted to her, "A whistlin' woman and a cacklin' hen, never come to a good end." Of course, Wootsie didn't pay any attention to him and carried on just as she had been. Wootsie even taught me how to whistle, and I still love doing it.

Wootsie was big-bosomed and attracted attention from Black and White men. She used their attraction to her to advance her interests. Men followed her around, but she had no intentions of marrying any of them because she wasn't going to mind any of them. That didn't stop the suitors from pursuing her, though. She was straightforward, direct, and no-nonsense.

Christine was boy-crazy as a teenager but Wootsie was hell-bent on keeping her in check. Once, Christine was about to walk down to the mailbox to meet a boy, and Wootsie asked,

"Where you goin' gal?" Christine said,

"I'm goin' down to the mailbox and someone's gonna pick me up."

"No you not. You tell whoever is comin' to meet you to come up here, so I can see 'em. You ain't goin' down to that road."

Wootsie stood guard over the teenage girls' virtue at the Hollow. There was no such thing as us running the streets when she was around.

Before I left for Virginia Union, Wootsie called me downstairs to the kitchen. She drank Country Club Malt Liquor in the little short cans. She popped open a can and poured it in her teacup. She then opened another can and poured it in a glass. "Drink it," she said. I was startled and said, "Really!?"

"Yeah, drink it. Drink all of it." After a few sips, I told her,

"This tastes awful. I don't wanna drink no more."

"I don't care. Drink all of it." About three quarters of the way through the drink, she said, "College gals don't know what being tipsy or drunk looks and feels like and that's how they get themselves in trouble and get raped. Drink all that beer," she insisted. After I finished the can, Wootsie asked,

"How's that top lip feelin'?"

"It feels right numb."

"Uh huh. Now you tipsy. Now that you know what it feels like. Remember it. When you feel like that, you hold your beer for the rest of the night. I don't care what party you go to. Don't put your beer down. Don't let nobody hold it for you. Take it with you even if you go to the bathroom, but don't drink no more. If someone offers you another drink, you tell 'em, 'No, I got one.' That way nothin' will happen to you." Wootsie taught me a valuable lesson. I taught the same lesson to my niece April when she was about to go to Union. I knew my oldest niece Melinda wasn't much for drinking, so I didn't bother with her.

As the youngest of Momma and Poppa's children, Wootsie was the rebellious type. She loved her parents, but she and Poppa clashed over several things because she was such a free spirit. Wootsie wore culottes frequently, but as far as Poppa was concerned, they were still pants. He was an old-time religious type, very traditional about what women did and didn't do, including what they should and shouldn't wear. He even took a position on how long a woman's skirt should be. If it was left up to Poppa, he would have gotten out a tape measure to make sure skirts were the right length. Wootsie, of course, didn't have any of it. "That's not the way it is now," was her response when she and Poppa got into it.

"You can't live like dat and get into heaven," he'd tell her.

"I'll get in, or just maybe, I won't go to no heaven."

It even shocked Momma Rosie when Wootsie said such things, but she just kept quiet while Wootsie went about her business. I believe Wootsie could sometimes be defiant just to be defiant. She smoked Salem cigarettes right in Poppa's presence instead of doing it behind his back, like Grandma Dollie would have done if she had smoked.

Following in the footsteps of her sisters and brothers, Wootsie completed the seventh grade. She too became a domestic, cleaning White folks' houses and looking after their children.

Once, Wootsie brought home a live possum in a box with the intention of fattening it up so we could eat it for dinner. By then we had a refrigerator, so the old icebox was empty and we used it as a storage bin. Wootsie put the possum in a section of the bin and placed a board inside to prevent it from biting her. She then filled up a small container of buttermilk and cornbread for the possum to eat. Every day she gave that possum water and the buttermilk-cornbread mixture to fatten it up and clean out its system. One day I followed her and asked what she was doing. She told me she was going to feed the possum. I asked if I could go with her, and Wootsie nodded yes. She told me:

"You know gal, possums are magic. If you tell a possum you gonna kill it and eat it, it'll disappear."

"Really!?"

"Absolutely."

I watched her put the buttermilk-cornbread mixture and water in for the possum and replace the top back on the old icebox and we left. Of course, I made a U-turn and went right back to the old icebox and raised the lid. That possum looked up at me, bared his teeth, and assumed a defensive stance. I told the possum, "Wootsie gon' kill and eat 'chu'." The possum just hissed and continued showing its teeth. I put the lid back down and put the brick back on top. I thought to myself, "If it's really magic, it'll go away now." I didn't want to eat such an ugly animal in the first damn place. The following morning, I found Wootsie downstairs in the kitchen cursing like a sailor about somebody letting her "damned" possum go. I started laughing, thinking to myself that the magic had actually worked.

Wootsie said, looking in my direction, "It was you!" She must have seen the guilt in my eyes. Wootsie wasted no time getting a switch and whipped me around in a circle. I probably didn't put the top down right and the possum escaped. I didn't want to eat that big-ass rodent anyway and was glad it got away.

Wootsie eventually married, but not until she was much older. As I recall, she was about fifty-nine at the time. She married a man named Ruben Chaney. Wootsie was his second wife. He had been interested in Grandma Dollie, but she wouldn't give him the time of day, so he turned his attention to Wootsie. He was a real sweet man, but he also drank a lot. He wasn't a drunk, but he drank more than he needed to. They stayed together until Wootsie died. Because he was so helpful, Grandma Dollie let him stay on at the Hollow. He continued to help out and even helped me when I started farming at Koehler. Eventually, Ruben married another woman in Martinsville.

Wootsie's chain smoking became her undoing because she eventually developed lung cancer. I was working at Miller and Christine was working at Fieldcrest Mills at the time. She and I took turns taking Wootsie for her chemotherapy treatments in Danville because neither Wootsie nor Grandma Dollie ever drove. Wootsie didn't spend much time in the hospital because Dollie took care of her. The chemotherapy and eventually the radiation treatment caused Wootsie to lose her mind. Those drugs robbed her of her senses. I'm not a fan of either of these treatments. You take them and you still die.

My former housekeeper, Mrs. Mattox, received the same diagnosis as Wootsie several years ago. She was advised that she would be set up with a round of chemo followed by radiation therapy. She told the attending physician, "Now that's what you told both my sisters years ago and both of them died. Your chemotherapy and radiation didn't save them. I don't mean to be rude, but I'm not doin' anything other than goin' home. If it gets really bad, I might come by to get a pain pill, but I don't want you to touch me." As I said, that was several years ago and she only recently stopped cleaning my house once a week. That was because she had a mild stroke.

Wootsie and Grandma Dollie were very close. They were like me and Christine. When Doretha mistreated Dollie,

Wootsie would step in and break them up. She was only some-what sympathetic to Doretha's perceived hurt, but Dollie was her sister, and she loved her sister. Wootsie was the balance. She'd tell her sister, "Oh Dollie, you know Doretha ain't got good sense," or "Doretha, you ain't gotta say everything that comes to yo' mind, gal. It just ain't necessary." That's how Wootsie intervened.

By 1985, however, Wootsie had become so sick from the can-cer that she needed round-the-clock attention. Grandma Dollie was right there as Wootsie's nurse and protector. It was also an opportunity for her to say goodbye to her youngest sister. In those last days, Wootsie hallucinated and had night terrors. She'd scream and holler that there were dogs under her bed and foxes in her room. I remember sitting beside her bed when she had an outbreak. Reading the Bible to her appeared to calm her down when she had an outburst. She became delusional and didn't even recognize her husband toward the end. Wootsie's last days were spent in terror. She'd scream out, "There's dogs in the house! There's dogs in the house! There's wolves under my bed. One nearly bit me!!" Grandma Dollie slept right beside her in the bed. She seemed to be the only one who could calm Wootsie down when her periodic outbursts occurred. She'd wrap her arms around her younger sister and would say, "Calm down Wootsie. Calm down, Baby. It's okay." Hearing her sister's voice right beside her, Wootsie usually settled down. There was no one better for Wootsie than her older sister, but it was painful for Grandma Dollie to see her baby sister decline in such a manner.

Wootsie eventually went into a coma, and we had to call an ambulance to take her to Martinsville Memorial Hospital. She only spent three days there before passing away. Over those three days, Dollie, Christine, and I took turns sitting with her. Wootsie had tried to die on the second day. I knew she was leaving us because her pulse and other vital signs were slowing down. I started crying and I grabbed her hand, pleading with her, "Wootsie, please don't die, please! We need you, Baby." Her pulse began to pick back up. Christine spent that night and I was coming in to relieve her. Christine was also going to pick up Grandma Dollie, but before she left, Christine told Wootsie, "I'll be leaving shortly, Baby, but Naomi will be here so I can go get Grandma Dollie." But before Christine left, Wootsie quietly slipped away. It all happened very quickly. Christine concluded that Wootsie wasn't going to die with me in the room, so she left before I got there. She knew I wouldn't take it well. To tell you the truth, I would have cried a river if it had kept her here.

When Wootsie died, Doretha was still living in Bassett. Grandma Dollie and I planned the funeral. Part of me was relieved that she was no longer in pain, because I honestly did not recognize that terrified woman who I had been looking at. Wootsie had been one of the strongest women I had known. Her death nearly broke my heart.

Having Wootsie around was like having two grandmothers. You had one for all the kisses and hugs and the other, fun one. At Halloween, for example, when we were young, she'd tell us, "Y'all chillun go on outside and play." Then she would put on a sheet and sneak out the back door and scare the daylights out of us in that sheet pretending she was a ghost. She also made us homemade Halloween candy because we couldn't go trick-or-treating as the only Black kids in the area.

I dream about Wootsie sometimes, and I always wake up with a smile afterward. I sometimes wonder what she would have been like as an old woman. It's hard for me to imagine her at an advanced age because she was so full of life. I do know that my Aunt Wootsie displayed that family grit that we were known for.

In my later life, when it was necessary for me to take a stand on an unpopular position as president of the NAACP, I feel Wootsie's spirit is with me. It was like she'd say, "Gal, don't let anyone boss you around. You stand up and go ahead." I am a better woman because of her.

8

Uncle Ramey and Aunt Alice

My great-uncle Raymond Finney was a handsome and very vain man. He was a dapper dresser and had a roving eye when it came to women. Uncle Ramey was self-centered and probably a little egotistical. He was also the hardest-working man I have ever known. He really was his father's son on steroids when it came to his work ethic. When Uncle Ramey was fifteen years old, he worked in the furniture factory for a short while and left vowing he would never work for White folks again. He kept that vow.

There had been persistent whispers that he was Momma Rosie's out-of-wedlock child because his complexion and hair was different from Poppa's, but as far as Poppa was concerned, that was his boy, and he was raised accordingly. These White/Black "relationships" were well known in Henry County. Black men were often forced to accept biracial children as theirs with an explanation from the wife that her great-grandmother was also light-skinned or some other manufactured explanation. Husbands learned not to question these situations and left well enough alone rather than face the harsh reality. If this was the case with Uncle Ramey, it, like many other issues, wasn't spoken of.

Uncle Ramey built a store in Bassett, Virginia, which was the anchor of his entrepreneurial activities. He cultivated gardens and sold all kinds of vegetables out of his store. Ramey also raised hogs and cows and butchered them to sell the meat. He always maintained four or five cows from which he produced milk, butter, cheese, and other dairy foods. He was a proper businessman down to his bones.

Ramey built a thick chest that he bolted to the joists of his building's floor so it couldn't be lifted. His wife, Aunt Alice, knew about the chest, but only Uncle Ramey had the key to the lock. After he passed away in the early 1980s, we discovered the chest was full of change. There were several thousand dollars' worth of nickels, dimes, and quarters in it. He had accumulated those coins over the sixty years he ran that store.

Uncle Ramey loved his parents, especially Momma Rosie. Those two had a special bond. He often picked her up and took her to church on Sunday. They were both relatively quiet people. Alice was jealous of the relationship that Ramey had with his mother. I remember when Momma Rosie passed away in 1968, Alice put some bright red lipstick on her mouth while she was in the casket. Momma Rosie would have never been caught wearing such a thing in life. She would have seen such an adornment as vain, and she was nothing like that. Uncle Ramey got upset with Alice for doing that, and Wootsie or Grandma Dollie removed the lipstick from their mother's remains.

While Uncle Ramey had a good relationship with Momma Rosie and Poppa, he was somewhat detached from his brothers (including Uncle Reely, who was raised as his brother) and sisters, because he always thought they were going to beg him for something. He was, by far, the most financially successful. In later years, he would come up to the Hollow for Sunday dinner and would sit and talk with Momma Rosie and Poppa as long as the road was dry. He didn't like getting mud on his tires. He also watched *Mutual of Omaha's Wild Kingdom* with us but wasn't that talkative. Uncle Ramey gave us Dentyne chewing gum which came in individually wrapped paper.

I earlier said Uncle Ramey had a roving eye when it came to women. Let me clarify a few things. He loved his wife, Aunt Alice, but I believe men can compartmentalize loving someone and being faithful to them. He went to barber school in West Virginia, but knowing Uncle Ramey, he had several side deals going on during his stay there. He and Alice stayed in West Virginia for a time, and then came back to set up his store and other business interests in Henry County.

The couple settled in Bassett. He built a large, two-story structure with a barbershop, a beauty parlor, a grocery store, and a restaurant on the first floor. The second level had a hotel where he rented rooms for people to stay. He rented mostly to single teachers who lived in the area. My uncle and aunt also built their personal home across the road overlooking their store.

Uncle Ramey occasionally visited his older sisters. Virginia Mae, or "Ginny Mae" as she was known, lived in Bluefield, West Virginia. Another sister, Emily, lived in Roanoke. Those were the siblings to whom he was the closest. I didn't really know either of these aunts as I was growing up. They only occasionally came to the Hollow. When Momma Rosie passed away, they were there by her bedside.

Years later, Grandma Dollie and Wootsie asked me to take them to Bluefield to see Aunt Ginny Mae. The three of us first drove to Roanoke to pick up Aunt Emily and then we drove to Bluefield. She was in failing health at the time and mostly sat in a chair throughout our weekend visit. Aunt Ginny Mae passed away not too long after that. I took them all back for her funeral. Within six months, Aunt Emily became ill and Wootsie was diagnosed with lung cancer. Emily passed away before Wootsie, but we didn't tell her about Aunt Emily's death, fearing it would worsen Wootsie's condition.

Grandma Dollie and Wootsie had another sister, Anna B. Finney, known as "Annabelle," who died of a bowel obstruction in 1936, the same year that Grandma Amy passed away. Poppa didn't have a church funeral for Aunt Annabelle. He told her while she was alive, "If you won't walk into a church, I won't be rollin' you in one." Accordingly, Annabelle had a graveside burial at Mountain Top Cemetery.

The seventh grade was as far as the typical black person went educationally throughout most of Virginia unless they used personal funds to attend high school. That seventh-grade education was enough for someone to have learned how to read, write, and do basic math. In other words, it was enough education to allow the average person to function in society. Ramey worked for a while after finishing school and may have farmed for some time before leaving the area.

In the early 1930s, Doretha started school in Bassett and lived with Uncle Ramey and Aunt Alice for several years until Uncle Sunny Boy got old enough to attend school. I think Poppa and Momma Rosie kept Uncle Sunny Boy home until he was seven because he was so small. Even though he was kept home, Poppa home-schooled Uncle Sunny Boy and when he began his formal education, he started at a third-grade level which placed him in the same grade as his older sister. Poppa had Sunny Boy reading and doing math at an advanced level for his age. He had also inherited his mother's phenomenal memory and could retain minute details.

After he married Alice, Uncle Ramey had an out-of-wedlock daughter named Sharon. Ramey and Alice did not have children together. Although Ramey had occasionally "stepped out" when it came to other women, Alice wasn't much better. She, however, only flirted with other men. Uncle Ramey took things further, which is how he ended up with Sharon.

People came from all over town to Uncle Ramey's place, because it was the only social outlet for Black people in the

Bassett area. They could get their supplies, socialize, and catch up on the latest gossip at the same time. In addition to the restaurant, there were two pool tables which also drew men into the establishment.

My first-grade schoolteacher, Miss McCabanis, was one of Uncle Ramey's renters. Uncle Jordan, Momma Rosie's nephew, lived there a while before he grew too out of control. Ramey had to put him out, which is when Jordan came to Koehler and lived in Grandma Dollie's house. Uncle Ramey and Aunt Alice had several income streams, but in his later years he became diabetic and had to cut back on some of his business ventures.

Alice's foolish behavior and meanness knew few bounds. It was Alice who taught Doretha much of her destructive behavior while she lived with Ramey and Alice off and on during her formative years. In fact, I am certain it was Alice who caused Doretha to act so recklessly throughout much of her adult life. Doretha idolized Alice.

Aunt Alice also sabotaged the relationship between Uncle Ramey and his daughter, Sharon. Alice allowed her to be disrespectful to her daddy with impunity. Once, I was in Uncle Ramey's car with him and Sharon and she knocked his hat off and called him a "knucklehead." I braced myself, because I was sure she was going to get an ass whippin' or at the very least a good and proper slap. He just got his hat and put it back on his head without saying a word. Bad parenting is an abomination. It often can't easily be undone. Once you've taught a child horrible things, you should expect that there will be consequences.

Doretha died pulling stunts and trickery. We could have lived at Koehler Hollow, but she pulled shenanigans because she wanted her criminal son, Terry, to stay there. She lamented on her deathbed that she wanted to go back to Koehler Hollow. Underhandedness and deceit will eventually come back to you. When it came to the kinds of untoward antics that Grandma Dollie knew her daughter was capable of, she had a saying, "You will see it on your plate, and you will sop it in your gravy." In other words, you will have to eat every bit of wickedness and wrongdoing that you put out to others.

The same crap that Alice taught Doretha as a child, she had to deal with for the rest of her life. Despite the fact that Alice and Dollie were best friends, Doretha was often with Alice when she was young, while Grandma Dollie was off working to support her children and eventually her grandchildren. You would think there would have been some resentment from Dollie toward Alice for negatively influencing her daughter, but there wasn't. I think once Doretha showed her mother how much she disliked her, Grandma Dollie kind of tuned her out. Once when she was a child, Doretha took a new dress that Dollie had bought and put it up in the chimney and got soot all over it. She did it to prevent Grandma Dollie from going out. I think at a point Dollie just adopted a position that she would do what she could for Doretha, but she wasn't going to let her daughter break her heart. Grandma Dollie was like that. As emotionally violent as Doretha could be, Grandma Dollie was mostly resigned that little could be done to improve what became a very toxic relationship.

It was Poppa and his best friend, Marshall Hairston, who made a mistake by not letting Dollie and Marshall's son, Jesse Ben, marry. He and Dollie had fallen in love when she was fifteen and Jesse Ben was nineteen. It wasn't a matter of Dollie's age as you might imagine. At the time, girls could marry as early as thirteen if they were deemed "mature" enough. Dollie and Jesse Ben's crime was that they were second cousins. The unofficial bloodline barrier that was not to be crossed was third cousins. After Dollie got pregnant by Jesse Ben, Poppa and Marshall Hairston should have just helped them to build a little house and stay together. As I said, they were in love. Had Dollie and Jesse Ben been allowed to marry, it could have changed everyone's life. Instead, Jesse Ben was sent off and because they were forced apart, Dollie had an out-of-wedlock child. The embarrassment of that caused Doretha to engage in recklessness throughout much of her life.

Jesse Ben Hairston was able to recoup his reputation from his "mistake." While Grandma Dollie was stuck in Henry County as an unwed mother, Jesse Ben married and had a son with his first wife. There was a definite double standard where women were concerned.

* * * * * * * * * * *

Uncle Ramey put you in mind of Floyd on the *Andy Griffith Show*. He was a light, brown-skinned man and had a premature white streak in the front of his head. He also had a widow's peak, and was quite handsome.

Alice was also a very pretty woman with a light complexion and was made up from the floor up like Dollie Parton. She had a head full of red hair with an ample bosom. She had accented that part of her body with breast pins even when she was a young woman and loved showing them off. Alice also loved going to parties.

After Uncle Ramey finished barber school, he and Alice moved back home where he opened a barbershop in Bassett. They were beyond prosperous as far as the Black community was concerned. They were considered upper middle-class. Uncle Ramey was also a very shrewd investor and saved his money meticulously.

Uncle Ramey's barbershop was also a general store with a restaurant, which in the Black community was something like what you would see on *The Waltons*. He and Alice also sold bootleg under the counter. Uncle Ramey repeatedly told Alice to be discreet about selling her bootleg because everybody in this part of Virginia who had two pennies to rub together made extra money by selling liquor. He said, "Look here Alice, don't sell dis' here liquor to nobody dat you don't know." That was the case when he left town on some business in West Virginia one day around 1937.

Aunt Alice was babysitting Doretha on this occasion when a good-looking Black fella came in the store. He turned out to be an undercover government agent rooting out bootleggers. Back then, they called them "tightropes" (implying they could hang you). Doretha said he was a tall, slender man. He wore a gray suit and an FDR summer hat to top things off. In other words, this man was clean. He was the type of person who Alice liked to flirt with.

This undercover agent asked Aunt Alice for a fifty-cent shot of liquor. Alice didn't know this man from Adam. Doretha knew she didn't know this man because she knew everyone who frequented their store, and this man was definitely a stranger. Alice had emptied the liquor out of the quart jars into a bucket and put the bucket underneath the counter where the cash register was. The counter had stools you could sit on in the front just in case you wanted to order a meal. Whether Alice was flirting or being smart, I don't know which. She went over to the bucket, sloshed him out a drink and slid the glass down the counter like you would see at a bar in a Western movie. The stranger downed his liquor, put his fifty cents on the counter, tipped his hat and walked out.

No more than an hour later, the police showed up and arrested Aunt Alice for selling bootleg. The undercover agent must have told them where they could find her stash, because they confiscated the bucket of liquor. Aunt Alice was put in jail in Martinsville. She was jailed for two or three days before the trial. Uncle Ramey, in the meantime, had come back to town. He was decked out in a three-piece suit when he arrived in the courthouse for Alice's trial. He had Doretha with him. Grandma Dollie, being the Christian woman she was, went to the jailhouse to comfort Aunt Alice. Her "comforting" included slipping a pint of liquor to her through the prison bars in the jail cell. Aunt Alice had a few nips before she got to court. Back then, the courthouse seat was in the center of town on the main street and the jail was in the basement. Those incarcerated could look through the small windows in the cell and see people's feet as they walked by. People could also slip contraband through those windows to those who were being held for trial if they happened to be unlocked.

Old Judge McBride heard Aunt Alice's case. Doretha said he had a pox-face that looked like he had had bad acne as a child and a great big nose like W. C. Fields. In other words, he was not a very attractive man. As Aunt Alice's case was called, she stumbled to the front of the courtroom. Old Judge McBride looked at her and said, "Gal, how many times I don' seen you in here? You been in here a few times of late." Having had a snout full of bootleg, Alice did not appreciate him calling her "gal." Doretha said she remembered Aunt Alice turning red when the judge was speaking to her, so she knew Alice was about to act up. Old Judge McBride then said, "Well gal, I'm gwine have to give you some time." Aunt Alice stood tall, put her hands on her swaying hips, and said lasciviously in her tongue-tied voice, "If I can't *pull it*, I'll get behind it and push it.[1] I ain't afeared of you." As she was talking to the judge, she swayed her curvaceous body around and threw out her ample bosom at the judge as she said, "*push* it." Uncle Ramey,

---

[1] "Pulling time" was a Southern expression for being incarcerated and serving the sentence.

Plate 1. Amy Finney Finney (circa 1910s).

Plate 2. Re-created painting of George Washington Finney.

Plate 3. George Washington Finney (circa 1910s).

Plate 4. George Washington Finney (circa mid-1950s).

Plate 5. James Cabel Finney (circa 1910s).

Plate 6. Loretta, David, and Naomi (circa 1956).

Plate 7. Loretta, Sharon (Uncle Ramey's daughter),
Christine, Naomi, and David (circa 1963).

Plate 8. Naomi as a nine-year-old.

Plate 9. Grandma Dollie (circa 1970).

Plate 10. Doretha.

Plate 11. Aunt Alice and Uncle Ramey (circa late 1940s).

Plate 12. Uncle Sunny Boy (circa mid-1960s).

Plate 13. Pokechop (circa 1965).

Plate 14. Doretha and Pokechop (circa late 1960s).

Plate 15. Doretha and Naomi at Maury Mill
on Blue Ridge Parkway (circa 1980).

Plate 16. Naomi Hodge-Muse (recent picture).

who was sitting in the back of the courthouse with Doretha, was so embarrassed at his wife's statement he just slid down in his seat. Old man McBride lost his temper. He banged the gavel down so hard the head flew off. "I'm not gon' have this, gal. I'm not gon' have this. You gon' serve ten days." So Aunt Alice had to serve ten days in jail for disrespecting the court in Henry County. That just shows you this contempt or lack of being intimidated just runs in our family.

I talked to Aunt Alice not long before she passed away. She was close to ninety years old. I asked her about her proclivity to get in trouble when she was a young woman. In fact, when she got drunk, she wanted to do one thing—fight. She and Uncle Ramey battled it out on many occasions. Once Uncle Ramey got mad and shot up through the floor. Of course, he didn't hit her. Another time, she got mad and shot down the hill at him. She didn't hit him either. They were truly an unlikely duo. Ramey was quiet, reserved, and gentlemanly. Alice was vivacious and out of control most of the time. What they shared in common was a love of making money and they did so quite well. They also loved each other. Aunt Alice rose every morning before the crack of dawn to get down to her store to open the restaurant. She fed the workers going off to work at the Bassett Furniture Factory.

Aunt Alice was Grandma Dollie and Uncle Ramey's third cousin. When Ramey was twenty-nine and Alice was thirteen, she ran away from home to find him in West Virginia while he was in barber school. Ramey started by cutting coal miners' hair. He was so enterprising that he cut hair and shaved corpses in preparation for their funerals. Not many barbers were willing to do that, but Uncle Ramey did so willingly because he received triple his normal fee for preparing dead bodies for public viewing. He cut the hair of Black and White bodies—it didn't matter to him. All he saw was green.

In any case, after Alice found Uncle Ramey, they formally married when she was fifteen. She then became Alice Finney Finney. Alice was a lighter-skinned woman with full lips. She always wore red lipstick. Aunt Alice also dyed her hair red which seemed to match her hair-trigger temper. She had a pronounced speech impairment. She couldn't move her tongue back and forth very easily the way other people could, so when she spoke, she had a pronounced lisp. When she was drinking, and that was often, Alice had alcohol-smelling breath that lingered. Anytime she went to a house party, Alice said the first thing she would do was to look around to see what she could grab ahold of to use as a weapon in case a fight broke out. In short, Alice Finney Finney was as crazy as a bedbug, but Doretha adored her. In fact, Alice would come up to Koehler and get Doretha as a little girl and keep her for extended periods of time. They formed the only real mother/daughter relationship Doretha had. When Doretha was young, she went to school in Bassett, where Uncle Ramey and Aunt Alice lived and ran their businesses.

Both Alice and Ramey did hair. Alice also cooked in the restaurant. She took meals up to the factory and sold them.

Uncle Ramey's store had two pool tables and a jukebox, and he also sold candy to the kids in the area. Their store became a gathering place.

By the time I came along they weren't selling liquor, but they still had several thriving businesses. Men waited patiently for upwards of three hours or more to get their hair cut or get in that shave. Uncle Ramey was cutting hair so often, many of his regulars lined up before he opened his shop. Those who waited didn't mind because it gave them a chance to gossip. Uncle Ramey had a number system, which meant those waiting could play pool, shop, or have a meal. Once Ramey called that customer's number, that man had three minutes to be in that chair or they would lose their place in line. He could have easily had two or three more barbers in there with him, but I think he was too stingy to share the profits with anyone.

Aunt Alice got up early in the morning and started cooking for those factory workers who might be single. She could provide them with breakfast before they started their shifts. She started in the kitchen at 4:00 AM. By 5:00 or 6:00 AM she had the bacon and sausage ready. She made bacon-and egg and sausage-and-egg sandwiches for pick up, and many of the factory workers did just that.

Uncle Ramey's daughter, Sharon, was three years younger than me. She was Uncle Ramey's biological child, but not Alice's. Still, Alice wanted to raise this little girl, but that relationship was strained at best. Alice resented the fact that the baby wasn't hers, especially since she wanted children so badly. But as it turned out, Alice was barren. Every time she looked at Sharon, she was reminded of Ramey's infidelity.

Aunt Alice routinely asked Doretha to give her one of us to raise. I was about eight when Doretha sent me to Bassett to live with Uncle Ramey and Aunt Alice. It was after my fourth bout of pneumonia. She believed Ramey and Alice's house was a better environment because it was larger and had central heating, indoor plumbing, and other amenities.

Living with them was fun at first, but then I discovered how mean Aunt Alice could be. I saw how she treated Sharon. At five years old, Sharon was a bedwetter, which is not unusual for a child that age. Aunt Alice would go into a raving fit when Sharon peed the bed. Alice beat Sharon while she cleaned her up. I witnessed those scenes and I said to myself, "This woman is insane. I am not stayin' here."

I had been with my aunt and uncle for about two weeks before Doretha came to check on me. As I said, she thought being in a larger home setting with central heat and no wood stove would be better for me. When Doretha came, I went slam off, screaming and hollering, "I wanna go home!" I even fell out on the floor flailing my arms and legs to make the point. I was thinking to myself, "I don't want to stay with this crazy-ass woman. I don't care about using a slop jar. I'll go gladly back to the outhouse." I saw what Alice had been doing to Sharon and I thought if I stayed there much longer, she'd turn her attention to me and give me the same treatment. Well, my tantrum worked, and Doretha took me out of there. When we were outside, she told me, "I ain't never seen you act like that before. It was so embarrassin'." I thought to myself, "Too bad, I'm not stayin' with that crazy woman."

That unhealthy relationship between Alice and Sharon continued. It was a classic love/hate scenario. It was love in front of the world where Alice was concerned, but behind closed doors Alice was another character. She bought Sharon a Volkswagen Beetle when she turned sixteen but treated her horribly when she was home. After she became grown, Sharon married and had two children. Alice doted on Sharon's son, Tyson, but he had a penchant for getting into trouble and was eventually incarcerated.

Alice also drove like a maniac, which was another reason why I didn't want to stay with her years earlier. She always kept a late-model car from when she was young, but when she was behind the wheel she saw no shoulders or dividing lanes. My aunt drove however the hell she wanted as long as it was fast. Alice got herself crippled up when she was going to pick up Tyson from a high-school basketball game and went around a curve too fast. She lost control of her car and ran right into the Smith River. Fortunately, there were witnesses around to call the police, or she might have drowned. The emergency services had to employ a lifesaving crew to get her out of the water. Alice was taken to the hospital and was there for at least a week.

Because Uncle Ramey had been a successful entrepreneur for most of his life, Alice also enjoyed a lifestyle well above most Black people in Henry County. Even after Ramey's death in 1982, she continued to run his various businesses and did quite well.

Aunt Alice could be jealous of other people's success though. For example, when I graduated from Union and got my first job at DuPont, she could hardly stand it. She had always been the big fish in the family. She and Ramey were the ones with the deep pockets. They were the ones who family members went to begging for money or asked to cosign on a loan. Alice enjoyed that position in the family. As far as she was concerned, we were her poor cousins from the Hollow. When Doretha told her about my progress or other accomplishments, Alice would change the subject. Doretha loved Alice, so the jealousy was somewhat subdued in my case. Alice also loved Doretha, so she wouldn't do anything to overtly antagonize their relationship.

When we were young, Alice even taught her daughter Sharon some of her selfishness and poisonous condescension. More than once, Sharon came up to the Hollow to play with us when she was a little girl and called us "poor niggas," but we knew she was only repeating what she had heard from Alice. She had also said we had rats and roaches, but none of that was true. The things that girl said were outrageous. We didn't like her that much when she was young. One time Sharon came with a big bag of candy that Aunt Alice had given her to share with us. But for us to get a piece of candy, we had to damn near kiss Sharon's ass. She expected us to beg her. Poppa and Momma Rosie had taught us to never beg, so we just left Sharon and her bag of candy alone.

Before Loretta died, she, David, Christine, and I had built a treehouse up in the woods and went off to play in it. We left Sharon and her candy behind at the main house. Of course, she followed us. We had a trapdoor in the treehouse. I had thrown a tarp over the trapdoor and said, "Hey Sharon, come over here and let me show you somethin'." Before Sharon got to the covered trapdoor, "Miss Goody Two-Shoes" Christine knew what I was up to and stopped Sharon from stepping on the tarp. Had she done so, she would have fallen out of the tree with her bag of candy. What I did was totally wrong, and I'm not proud of it, but I can't deny that it happened.

Of course, Sharon went straight back to the house and told on us. Alice told Doretha that we were trying to break her little girl's leg. She was half drunk by that time, but got out, "I'm a go up there an' burn that damn house down." Doretha spoke up at that point and said, "No you ain't, Alice. Loretta helped build that treehouse and you will not touch it. If your little girl wasn't actin' so hateful, these chaps wouldn't have tried to hurt her." Alice grabbed Sharon by the hand and staggered out of the house. She drove off drunk. It's a wonder she didn't get in another accident.

There was sometimes a strained dynamic between our family, Uncle Ramey, and Aunt Alice, because she could do some hateful things with no good explanation. Another example happened after Uncle Ramey died. I asked Alice to sell me his fishing gear, but she refused. She ended up giving it away instead of selling it to me. The same thing happened when I asked her to sell me his small tractor. She also gave that away. My gut told me she resented that I had a good-paying job at Miller Brewers by then and she was making sure that I wouldn't get anything she had control of.

Doretha, as I said, loved Alice and also delighted in some of her shenanigans. That's how Alice helped to twist Doretha up. She was a horrible role model for a little girl. My mother learned how to gossip, how to manipulate people, and how to do wrong to others. And it all came from Aunt Alice.

Years back, Doretha told me some thugs had beaten a man up and thrown him out of a car right below Uncle Ramey and Aunt Alice's house. They just threw him out in the road and left him. He was clearly injured. Most people would have called the police or offered the man some assistance, which is what Ramey did. But while Uncle Ramey went off to call the cops, Alice suggested that she and Doretha go down and kick his ass too. When I questioned Doretha why she would even consider doing such a thing, she said, "I don't know. It was just somethin' to do. I knew it was wrong. Anyway, Ramey stopped us before we got to him." That's the kind of behavior Alice was capable of and how she negatively influenced my mother.

Alice would even go to church half drunk, cussing people out. Once, she tried to put her lipstick on and missed her mouth by a mile even though she had beautiful, full lips. Oftentimes she'd stagger in church and fall asleep. Sometimes when she'd raise hell in the church, Christine would yell "Amen" very loudly to drown her out. It took her twenty years of staggering up those church steps half drunk before she finally got saved. She also stopped some of her horrible meanness. I see Alice's path to redemption as a lesson. Although it took years before she gave in to the Lord, she did it. And I loved her for that.

Even though Alice got saved in her later life, some of her past deeds came back to haunt her, specifically the troubled relationship she had created with her daughter Sharon. After Alice messed up her hip in the car accident, she had to stay in the downstairs part of her house. Sharon begrudgingly took Alice to visit her incarcerated son, Tyson, after Alice insisted on seeing him. This was the grandson that Alice had doted on and spoiled. After the visit, Sharon rarely stayed behind, which left Aunt Alice to make her way back into the house struggling.

Alice had another run-in with the law as an old woman. In addition to needing a walker to move around, she also developed a noticeable shake in her hand. It was a palsy which caused her right hand to involuntarily bob up and down. It was more than a tremor, but it did not stop Alice from managing her affairs. It just took her longer to do things. Sharon's estranged first husband, who we simply called "Squirt," once came into Alice's store. Those two didn't like each other from the beginning. Why he came to that store to antagonize his former mother-in-law, especially someone given to conflict as easily as Alice, was anybody's guess.

Squirt must have been in his mid-thirties when he entered that store cussing away. Alice, moving toward him on her walker, told him to get out of her shop. Alice said, "Looka here. I'ma Christian woman an I ain't havin' all that cussin' up in my store." Squirt defiantly responded, "Why don't you just shud' up, you ole bitch." Alice paused but kept moving toward Squirt on her walker. She stopped, reached down in her front apron pocket, and pulled out a pistol with her right hand shaking up and down. She said, "I ain't gon' be no bitch up in my store." Bam! She shot Squirt in the right leg. Fortunately for him, Alice shot him on the downstroke with her bobbing hand. Had she shot him on the upstroke, she could have hit one of his testicles. Squirt went down screaming in pain and shouting, "Oh God! This ole bitch shot me!" Another patron in the store called the police.

I was working at Miller at the time and was called to the phone with an emergency call. When I got to the phone and said hello, Grandma Dollie shouted, "Naomi!" I could hear the urgency in her voice which was very uncharacteristic of her.

"Yes, Grandma!? What's wrong?"

"Alice is in jail!"

"What!?"

"Alice's been arrested!"

"For what?"

"I don't know for sure. You gotta go an' bail her out. I hear tell she shot somebody."

I immediately thought to myself, "That's certainly plausible given Alice's history with guns." I left work and went to the

Henry County's Sheriff's office. When I arrived, one of my high school classmates, Herman Green, was fingerprinting Aunt Alice. He put her bobbing finger on the ink pad to place it, but because of her palsy she was hitting every spot but the sheet where her fingers were supposed to go. She got ink all over the desk. Herman was quietly laughing, but managed to say, "Miss Alice you can't put ink everywhere. You have to let me help you." Alice said, with her hand still jumping up and down, partly out of nervousness this time, "I'm doin' the best I can." I paid $250 bail to get her released.

Here in rural Virginia, things are handled a little less formally than in the large urban areas. Sometime after the shooting incident, the former Henry County prosecuting attorney, Bob Bushnell (who recently retired as a judge) paid a visit to Alice. His hair was blonde and frizzy like a Black person's. It was similar to Bob Ross, the artist's, hair. I was sitting on Aunt Alice's porch with her and Doretha. Bob Bushnell came up and said with a proper Southern drawl, "Y'all mind if I come up and talk to you a bit?"

Alice said, "Yes sir. Come on up."

"I'm Bob Bushnell and I am the prosecuting attorney. I just wanna know, Miss Alice, why'd you shoot that fella?"

Alice said, in total sincerity, "I'ma Christian woman. That man come up in my store callin' me an ole bitch. I ain't gon be no ole bitch up in my store." No doubt because of Alice's distorted tongue-tied delivery, Bob Bushnell's neck immediately turned red and then rose to his face. You could even see his scalp was red through his hair. He wanted to break out laughing, but he didn't. He could see Alice was totally serious.

When the case was called in court, Bob Bushnell must have spoken to the judge and explained things to him. I also suspect there wasn't much interest in putting a seventy-year-old woman in Alice's condition in jail. The judge asked Squirt if he had said what Alice had alleged and he confirmed it. The judge then said to Squirt, "You had no right goin' into this woman's place of business and callin' her a bitch. Also, when she ordered you to leave her store and you chose to remain, that made you a trespasser on her property." He struck his gavel on the block and said, "Case dismissed."

It was that area of the South where we lived where a prosecuting attorney could come speak to the perpetrator like that, but she didn't lie. Aunt Alice was definitely an acquired taste. You had to give her a dose of forgiveness because she wasn't always there mentally. At least that's what I told myself.

On another occasion, Doretha went to check on her when Alice hadn't answered her phone after several attempts. When Doretha arrived at the house, she smelled a foul odor coming from the house and suspected the worst. Instead, she found Alice lying in her own waste in her bed. Doretha contacted me and insisted we help her.

I went to buy Alice a new mattress and a box spring. I got a friend, June, to help Doretha and me with some of the heavy lifting. In addition to burning the old mattress, we decided to clean out all the debris in Alice's house. Once we got everything in a pile, we set it to light. The old waste-soaked mattress was totally destroyed. June put some kerosene on it and set all the debris on fire. I had gone back in the house but came back out when I saw June standing near the flame. I told him he'd better move away, because Alice had live shells among the debris we had collected in the house and some of them, no doubt, had landed in that fire. Not fifteen seconds had passed before some of those bullets started exploding. Both of us took cover and ran back in the house.

Aunt Alice became increasingly paranoid in her later years and always thought someone was trying to break in on her. I think it was Sharon's second husband who once paid Alice a visit one afternoon and found Alice holding one of her rifles when he arrived. In her tongue-tied lisp, she told him, "Some nigga was sneakin' 'round tryin' to break in on me, but I took care of that nigga. I tol' 'em, 'Nigga you be'd get from 'round here!' I heard where he was standing. He ain't move, so I shot 'em through my back door."

Sharon's husband went out to investigate to see who Alice had shot at. He stumbled onto a buck that was dead as hell. *That* was Alice's intruder, no doubt rummaging in her garbage cans for food in the backyard. After I heard that story, I called her on the telephone before I went to see her. The phone would ring twenty times before she got to it. By then, Alice's movement around on her walker was at a snail's pace. If you came up on her unannounced, there was a chance she would gut-shoot you.

If it hadn't been Doretha who discovered Alice in that condition, someone else would have. On that occasion, however, she had to be taken to the hospital where she underwent surgery. After she recovered, Alice was not allowed to return home and was sent to Blue Ridge Nursing Home in Stuart. I went there to visit Aunt Alice only to see that she had developed gangrene on her right foot. She didn't want to make a big deal about it, but I insisted it be treated. Alice eventually died of that infection in 2007.

9

Uncle Sunny Boy and the Martinsville Seven

Without question, my favorite uncle was James Alfred Finney, known to us as "Uncle Sunny Boy." He always smelled like Old Spice cologne. He was a big man and stood about five feet, eleven inches. He had wide shoulders and dimples on both cheeks. His complexion was honey brown and he was a very masculine man. Even as a child, Sunny Boy had a benevolence about him. When he came around, the atmosphere immediately brightened because he was always ready to smile and please people. It was like he brought fresh air into a room. Everyone saw it in him. He was never any trouble in school and all the teachers loved him. As a boy, he would walk around a room full of adults and reach out and shake hands with every single person without the slightest prompt. He impressed practically every adult he met.

He projected a kindness wherever he went. That's why we think God took him away from us so soon. Poppa gave him the nickname "Sunny Boy" because of his kind disposition. He was positive, upbeat, and happy. Grandma Dollie said she never knew a baby who smiled more than him. She also told me when he was a toddler, she would sometimes feign a frowned look at him and he'd look as if he was about to cry, because he thought he had done something wrong. There was another time that Dollie said she had to discipline him for something, which was a rare occurrence for this child. After a short while, Uncle Sunny Boy came back to his mother and told her, "I'll forgive you for beatin' me this time." Grandma Dollie said she had to stop herself from laughing. Uncle Sunny Boy was an easy-going child who rarely, if ever, gave adults any trouble. He became a very handsome young man and maintained his very confident smile.

When I was young, Uncle Sunny bought me a glass tea set and I treasured it for more than thirty years. I still had a piece of the original setting when I got married. Grandma Dollie broke it when she was using it as a sugar bowl. I was Sunny Boy's little girl. He'd pick me up and always had Juicy Fruit chewing gum in his pocket. He'd say, "Go in my shirt pocket baby girl. There's somethin' for you."

Sunny Boy was also a calming presence in the family. Momma Rosie adored this child and Grandma Dollie doted on him. Even the stern and formerly enslaved Grandma Amy privileged this great-grandson. He managed to soften her tough hide and she just couldn't resist giving in to him. According to Doretha, Grandma Amy was in one of her famous bad moods and Uncle Sunny Boy handed her one of his toys to brighten her up. The old lady's heart melted because he was no more than three or four at the time.

Sunny Boy grew into a generous man. He'd sometimes walk up behind Momma Rosie, kiss her on the cheek, and put a few dollars in her hand. Neither would say a word, but she would nearly be in tears at his generosity and giving spirit. There was a magical bond between those two.

Sunny Boy's older sister, Doretha, was also very close to her brother, but there was some obvious jealousy. Can you imagine Doretha, a difficult, strong-willed, combative, and manipulative child and Sunny Boy, who lived to please people? She thought he was a coward because, according to her, he was too easy-going and didn't have any fight in him. She thought he let people take advantage of him. She had fought several boys who wanted to mess around with her younger brother. Doretha wasn't having anyone maltreat him. Sunny Boy tried to get along with everyone and Doretha didn't give a damn about getting along with anyone. This brother and sister had completely opposite personalities, but she loved her little brother, nonetheless. She couldn't help but to.

While Grandma Dollie doted on her son, she never said who his daddy was. But he must have been handsome. I am not sure Uncle Sunny Boy ever asked his mother. It just wasn't spoken of. As far as male role models were concerned, however, Sunny Boy had Poppa as well as his uncles and cousins. Uncle Ramey once gave Sunny Boy a job in his store, but Alice caught him giving away food to someone who said they couldn't afford to pay. He was just too kind-hearted for words.

Uncle Sunny Boy was drafted as a young man and served in the U.S. Army as an infantryman. It's hard for me to imagine him on a battlefield unless he had been a medic or a corpsman. In any case, he dutifully served as a cook and was honorably discharged. He was posted to Germany for a while and told us stories about it when we were young.

Even with his compassionate disposition, Sunny Boy had his limits when it came to how he believed he should be treated. He worked for years at Blue Ridge Hardware store. In fact, he was such a dedicated and loyal employee he was heavily relied on. Sunny Boy knew the precise location of everything in the store. With his superior memory (a trait he inherited from his mother), he could easily direct customers to specific machine parts, cleaning supplies, or tools. He also became responsible for stocking and ordering equipment. When his manager retired, Sunny Boy easily stepped into the role and carried on without the slightest interruption. About four months into the job, however, the owner introduced him to a young White man. The owner then told him, "Sunny, you need to train this boy to become the manager of this store." Looking at the owner a little astonished, Uncle Sunny said, "Sir, I've been doin' this job for the last four months. I know where everything is in the store, and it has operated very smoothly. I thought I would continue doin' it." The owner looked at Sunny Boy with equal astonishment and said in a Southern drawl, "Sunny, you knows you's Colored. I can't have a Colored man as a permanent manager of this store." Polite, as always, Uncle Sunny said, "Well, sir, I thank you kindly, but I will not be trainin' another man to take the job I'm more than capable of handlin'. This will be my last day in your employ." Sunny Boy said the White owner stood there shocked with his mouth open, but never said another word. Uncle Sunny took off his apron, cleared out his locker, and left. It was that old Finney family grit that kicked in, once again. That White man felt sweet-natured Uncle Sunny Boy, who had served his country with distinction in the military, was not good enough to manage a hardware store. It was, of course, an insult to him. Uncle Sunny Boy told me that story when I was a teenager. I can't remember the context in which he told me, but I recall thinking back to when Poppa returned that eleven cents to Mr. Via after receiving too much change. That same swell of pride that I had for Poppa in that moment, I had for Uncle Sunny.

Sunny Boy then got a job as a chauffeur for former governor Thomas "Bahn" Stanley. He worked for him for several years. When he drove the governor to Florida, Sunny also worked as his cook.

Sunny Boy's compassion for people extended into his relationships with women as well. Neither of the women with whom he had long-term relationships with was worthy of him, I felt. The first relationship that I knew of was with a woman who already had several kids by other men. I think Sunny Boy pitied that woman and got into a relationship with her so she would have some companionship. Uncle Sunny Boy and the woman had a daughter, Jean. She was a few years younger than Christine. Jean's mother was also asthmatic. She suffered a severe attack and died. Of course, Sunny Boy got custody of his daughter, but for a short time considered taking custody of his girlfriend's other minor children until he realized that would be too much for him. He was that decent a man.

For a while, Uncle Sunny Boy and Jean lived with Grandma Dollie. Since she wasn't much younger than Christine, she often played with us. Then Sunny Boy married a woman, Roxie. She had been one of Wootsie's drinking buddies, but once again Sunny Boy seemed as if he needed to save this woman who clearly had a drinking problem. They bought a small house in Carver where Roxie helped Sunny Boy to raise his daughter.

The day Uncle Sunny Boy died was traumatic for everyone in the family. The day before, he had been at the main house in the Hollow lying down on the sofa watching television. He had been looking through the family photo album with Doretha and they were bringing up memories of Grandma Amy, Poppa, and other relatives whose pictures were in the book. Typically, he had kids there climbing all over him. He told Momma Rosie he was going home to rest, and he gave her a goodbye kiss, which she cherished from this grandson.

The following morning at about 6:00, we received a panicked call from Roxie telling us that Uncle Sunny Boy had collapsed. The paramedics came and diagnosed it as a heart attack. We were all nervous, trying to understand what that meant. A little later, word came that Sunny Boy was gone. Grandma Dollie fainted. Momma Rosie just shut her eyes tight and clenched her fists together as if it hadn't really happened. She just kept repeating, "Jesus, Jesus, Jesus, Jesus, Jesus . . . . ." The rest of us just cried in total disbelief. He was thirty-seven years old.

Because he was loved by so many people, Uncle Sunny Boy had a huge funeral. Some of his old army buddies came from out of state to pay respects. They had so many fond memories of their friend from the military. They told us how he had used his wit on several occasions to defuse tense situations among them. We all knew that was just like him. Many White people also came to his funeral, including former governor Bahn Stanley. He came up to Grandma Dollie and hugged her. They shared a good cry together. We were all impressed that our uncle had touched so many lives.

For some reason, I can't remember where Doretha was when we got the news of Sunny Boy's death, but she too was devastated. Somehow, she got it in her head that looking at that old family photo album had something to do with Sunny Boy's death. She was convinced that looking at those old pictures had somehow conjured up some bad spirit and doomed her brother. She forbade that album from being opened after his death, and it was kept closed and placed in a trunk in Koehler Hollow. No one saw that family photo album again until 2015, the year Doretha passed away. I saw it before she died, but even that had to be done in secret. I was afraid that had she known it had been opened, she would have flown off the handle. The shame of it is that many of the people in that photo album, which hadn't been opened to my knowledge since 1967, are now long gone. I don't know who many of them are, and those who could have identified them for me have all passed on. It's not likely I will ever know who many of those unknown smiling faces belong to. I might have been able to give a fuller picture had I known who many of those people were.

James Alfred "Sunny Boy" Finney became the latest ancestor to join other family members in eternal repose at Mountain Top Cemetery. His beloved grandfather George Finney, his great-grandmother Amy, his aunt Annabelle, and his niece Loretta were among the other family members already resting there. He was honored with a military burial along with an official burial marker. Unlike several other relatives, we know where his remains continue to rest.

Uncle Sunny Boy's daughter Jean was not yet a teenager when her father died. She became estranged from the family as an adult. She wanted her father's portion of Koehler Hollow to assist with her college education, but Grandma Dollie declined the request, telling her that would mean the property would have to be sold and she couldn't let that happen. Jean became embittered after that. As I recall, she didn't come to Grandma Dollie's funeral when she passed away in 1996. It baffled me that Jean would expect Grandma to sell the homestead to benefit her. I advised her to apply for financial aid as I had. She said she wasn't going into debt to go to Hampton University. It's likely that Roxie put her up to make the request of Grandma Dollie.

After Momma Rosie passed away in 1968, Grandma Dollie came down with spinal meningitis. The initial diagnosis was made at the hospital in Martinsville, but it became more severe, so she was referred to Duke University Hospital and almost died. I remember the time well because Grandma Dollie seemed resigned to her own death. Uncle Sunny Boy passing away the year before took Dollie to a dark place that we weren't sure she would make it back from. For an extended period, she moved in with Aunt Alice and Uncle Ramey. It was as if her spirit had left when her son died. With Momma Rosie gone and Grandma Dollie out of commission, that left me to take care of things in the household. Wootsie was away during the week working to keep money coming in. David, Christine, and I looked after Terry and got him ready, fed, and off to school. And then we had to go to school ourselves. Doretha was still working at Jobbers Pants Factory. She got up early to get a fire going before leaving for work. I made the other kids breakfast before we left. When Grandma Dollie recovered, she came back to help me, but it wasn't an easy time.

* * * * * * * * * * *

One of the most notorious events to come out of this region during Uncle Sunny Boy's short life was the infamous Martinsville Seven case. The result of that trial caused Sunny to join the military, which relieved Poppa to no end. His military service took him from this part of the state, and as far as Poppa was concerned, to his safety.

The Martinsville Seven case in 1949 rocked this entire region. Seven African American men were accused and "convicted" of rape and were electrocuted by the Commonwealth of Virginia. It shocked the nation and, in many ways, the world. All but one of them were young men in their twenties, and my uncle was friends with two of them. Their crime was the sexual assault of a White woman. Older people who were alive in the area at the time remember the case well. Many of them refused to talk about it because it was such a terrible experience for them. Those who spoke about it believe there was more to the story than what was reported in the papers. At least two generations of Martinsville natives have grown up whispering things or offering alternative theories about what took place back then.

Of course, this part of the country had a tradition of executing and lynching Black men for much less. But the truly damnable aspect of this American miscarriage of justice was that in 1949, Virginia law allowed for the imposition of the death penalty on Black men for raping White women. This death penalty standard did not apply to White men in the Commonwealth who committed rape against Black women. As you might imagine, a story as sensational as this also generated significant back chatter, particularly among African Americans in the area. I think it's important to know what we heard and what was said about this case. It will tell you something about the challenges we had to negotiate in this part of the state and how racial codes were enforced by statute.

The backdrop to this drama was an old Southern adage that an unobserved Black boy (or man for that matter) would commit rape at the slightest opportunity. Throughout the history of this country, African American boys have been warned by their fathers and mothers not to place themselves in situations where they could be accused of inappropriate contact with a White woman because it didn't take much for them to be found guilty of such an offense. In such instances, the young man was automatically assumed to be guilty. You need to know this, because as much as we have progressed, I fear some of these sentiments continue to linger.

In the early evening of Saturday, January 8, 1949, a thirty-two-year-old married White woman, Ruby Stroud Floyd, was in the African American section of Martinsville. She was known to proselytize in that part of town as a Jehovah's Witness missionary. On this occasion, she had been warned not to stay in the area too late as it might not be safe for her on a Saturday evening. But Floyd persisted, claiming she was in that section of town to collect on a debt. To assure her safety, she was accompanied by an eleven-year-old black boy, Charlie Martin, to escort her to the east Martinsville neighborhood.

Sometime later in the evening, a disheveled, bruised, and traumatized Ruby Floyd showed up at a Black family's house in the area pleading for help. An ambulance was sent for and the Martinsville police were also summoned. She told them she had been brutally attacked by several Black men. Based on her account, the police arrested twenty-year-old Frank Hairston, Jr., and twenty-two-year-old Booker Millner for the crime. Over the course of the evening, these two young men signed confessions of rape and implicated five others. Charlie Martin was brought to the jailhouse and placed the two detained men at the scene. In short order, Howard Lee Hairston (twenty), his brother James Hairston (twenty-two—neither related to Frank Hairston, Jr.), John Claybon Taylor (twenty-three), and Francis DeSales Grayson (thirty-eight) were arrested and implicated in the rape of Ruby Floyd. Within two days, Joe Henry Hampton (twenty-one), the accused initiator of the attack on Floyd, was the last of the seven to be apprehended. He had been the only one of the young men to have a serious police record.

The Honorable Kennon C. Whittle was the judge who oversaw the trials of the seven men in Martinsville. Although he made public pronouncements that race would not be a factor in the prosecution of the accused, it was, without question, the overarching dynamic surrounding the entire inglorious affair. Whittle dismissed defense efforts to move the trial to another location because of the sensationalism surrounding it. There were six separate trials. Two of the defendants, John Taylor and James Hairston, chose to be tried together. Although African

Americans had been in the jury pool, not a single one was selected to serve on a jury of the accused men. (The entire town only had eleven registered African American voters in 1946.)

The Martinsville Seven were judged by juries of all White men. The trials were held back to back with a separate jury deliberating for each of the defendants over eleven days. The prosecution called practically the same witnesses for each trial including young Charlie Martin. While he was on the stand, Charlie was asked questions like, ". . . do you know what happens to little boys who tell lies when they die?" He responded, "Yes, sir . . . they go to hell."[1]

The prosecution also produced physical evidence arguing that nonconsensual sex had taken place. Several of the defendants admitted having had sex with Floyd but said it had been consensual. Others asserted they never touched her. The admission of any kind of sex between a Black man and a White woman in 1949 rural Southwest Virginia automatically made the individual(s) guilty in the minds of the exclusively White male jurors.

Ruby Floyd, the key prosecution witness in each of the six trials, emotionally recounted her ordeal. Several of the defendants rejected parts of their confessions once taking the stand, stating that they had been coerced by the police without the benefit of a lawyer or a family member to advise them.

---

[1] Eric W. Rise, *The Martinsville Seven: Race, Rape, and Capital Punishment* was a helpful source in this chapter.

None of the trials lasted more than a full day. The delib-
erations for each trial lasted between thirty and ninety-seven
minutes. The outcome was predictable—all were found guilty
with a recommendation of capital punishment for the entire
Martinsville Seven.

In the aftermath of the verdict, the Virginia Conference of
the NAACP, along with several other civil rights organizations,
took up the cause of the seven men. Several high-profile civil
rights attorneys, including the late Oliver Hill and Martin A.
Martin, came in to take up the formal appeal. They challenged
the verdict on procedural issues, such as holding the trials on
successive days so close together, all but guaranteeing guilty
verdicts. The organization also argued that due process had
been overlooked along with other constitutional protections.

Other organizations, such as the Communist Party of the
United States, the International Labor Defense, and the Civil
Rights Congress, also entered on the side of the Martinsville
Seven appeal, but because of their leftist leanings or Communist affiliations were minimized by the cloud of the "Red
Scare" blanketing the country in the early 1950s. Protests were
staged in Richmond and elsewhere and international condemnation rained down on the Commonwealth because of the
verdicts. The case was argued before the Virginia Supreme
Court of Appeals which ultimately upheld the original verdict and sentences. The NAACP and the other Martinsville
Seven advocates fared no better in their appeals to the newly
installed Virginia Governor, John S. Battle, despite the fact his

office received thousands of letters pleading for clemency. The United States Supreme Court declined to hear an appeal.

In early February 1951, the seven men were put to death.

For most of their history, Virginia and other Southern states had executed Black men found guilty of raping White women. The Martinsville Seven were only the most recent to suffer the unfortunate Southern legal practice of enforcing codes of racial behavior.

The Black community in Martinsville viewed the entire saga through a different lens than the courts and passed those views down through the next two generations. In the immediate aftermath of the assault, African Americans became hypersensitive. Several Black men armed themselves and accompanied their wives, girlfriends, and children wherever they went because area White men had made noises that they were going to do the same thing to a Black woman that those boys had done to Ruby Floyd. Those who were young at the time remember being afraid of walking to school for fear of being attacked.

When the incident occurred, George Finney was well outside the age of suspicion at sixty-nine years old. Nonetheless, he armed himself like many other Black men when he left the Hollow. He was more concerned about his precious nineteen-year-old grandson, Uncle Sunny Boy. He could be targeted by Whites as a potential rapist. After all, he was in the same age range as the majority of those boys who were involved with the assault. In fact, Sunny Boy had known and been friends of the Hairston brothers. He couldn't imagine either of them being involved in such a horrific crime. Anyone who knew peace-loving Uncle Sunny Boy would have known that he would never have harmed a sparrow. He even detested hunting animals when Poppa taught him to do so as a boy. When Sunny Boy told Poppa he was thinking about joining the military, he quietly encouraged him to do so as a safeguard because he knew that would take him out of the Martinsville area. As it turned out, he was drafted.

Grandma Dollie was circumspect about the issue when she was doing domestic chores in White people's houses at the time. When her employers attempted to solicit her thoughts about the incident, she'd give a vague noncommittal response and keep quiet thereafter. Some well-meaning Whites knew Dollie had a teenage son and quietly suggested that he needed to keep a low profile while the area's racial tensions were high. Dollie quietly acknowledged their concerns and kept working.

Miss Alberta Wilson (who recently passed away at 101) was twenty-nine at the time and remembered the Martinsville Seven incident very well. She insisted they weren't wild boys. It was common knowledge in the Black community, according to her at the time, that Ruby Floyd had in fact been having an affair with Francis DeSales Grayson, one of the accused. Although he lived and worked in Martinsville without his wife and family, the father of five denied that he had sex with Floyd on the evening in question. The rumored sexual relationship between Floyd and DeSales Grayson was not explored during the trial because neither side saw any benefit in bringing it up.

The prosecution avoided it because it would have made Ruby Floyd appear even worse as a married White woman having an affair with a Black man. The defense wanted to avoid the subject for the same reason. Grayson's moral character would have sunk more deeply than it already had.

My future husband, Bill Muse, was the president of the NAACP in Martinsville in 1949 when the rape trial occurred. He remembered what took place that day. He told me Ruby Floyd had been in his office on the very afternoon of the assault. He remembered her acting in a flirtatious manner toward him in his office to the point where he had to put her out. Bill Muse told her she needed to leave that section of town because she had no business there. Floyd did not heed that advice. Bill Muse was not listed as a witness for either side, despite the fact that his testimony might have weakened the prosecution's case when it came to Ruby Floyd's character.

Bill, however, was among the community leaders and businessmen who were expected to tow the line of outrage at what these boys had been accused of. Some Black businessmen openly said that if the Martinsville Seven were fairly tried and convicted of the accused crime, they should face death. It was an old Southern self-preservation tactic. Some of these men were economically dependent on White patronage and support. For them, it was a matter of survival. However, several of those who publicly offered condemnation secretly funneled money to assist in the defense of the accused. Still, others assisted the families with burial costs once the inevitable occurred.

After the initial verdict in Martinsville, Bill was approached by a man representing the Communist Party offering to contribute money for the appeals of the seven men. This man believed America had been hypocritical by giving these men the death penalty when a murder had not been committed. In the end, however, Bill turned down the money, because as president of the Martinsville chapter of the NAACP, he didn't want to be associated with the Communist Party. The national office was eager to distance itself from leftist communist sympathizers.

The Black people of Martinsville, while shamed at what the seven were accused of, still held meetings and raised money for their defense. Outrage in the community was especially directed at DeSales Grayson, a relative newcomer to the town. Some argued that he was more responsible for what took place than his younger co-defendants. A twenty-year-old man, after all, was more likely to be "hot in the pants" than a man Grayson's age. Grayson, a World War II veteran, should have known better. Grandma Dollie, who was around the same age as Francis DeSales Grayson, shared this view and told Momma Rosie and Poppa that he came down to this area and stirred up "some mess." Doretha thought DeSales Grayson was attractive. She couldn't understand why he would go playing around with a married White woman when there were so many eligible Black women whom he could have dated.

After the appeals had been exhausted and sentences carried out, Miss Alberta attended some of the funerals of the seven. She remembered seeing a few of the bodies at the

James T. Allen Funeral Home. Grayson's remains stayed in Richmond, where all the executions had taken place. A Catholic, he was funeralized at St. Joseph's Catholic Church in Jackson Ward in Richmond.

Some of those executed boy's people are still around, but their parents are long gone now. Most of those boys were so young. Many who were kids at the time remember being at the funeral of the Hairston brothers. A few young people at the funeral remember a heavy rainstorm afterward as if some sort of punishment was being visited on the people for the unjust deaths of these brothers. It was scary for those who were there.

Stories also emerged about Judge Whittle, who oversaw the initial trial and handed down the death sentences. He developed a drinking problem, which many believed was related to the Martinsville Seven case. He lived in a plantation house known as Belleview in Ridgeway, Virginia. The domestic workers in his employ said he began seeing things. All agreed that he was a kind enough man, even going the extra mile to provide Christmas presents for the families of his Black domestic workers. But there was something about that house, according to several of those who maintained the residence. There was an unnatural presence in that place that several working there spoke about. Even after the house was sold to some people from New Jersey, reports emerged that the new residents heard horses running at night.

Judge Whittle went so far as to justify his actions in the Martinsville Seven case to his domestic workers. He reportedly said that all he did was follow the law. But that wasn't true. He was not obliged to give those boys the death penalty. He had sent a message to any Black man that this ". . . would be your fate if you were found guilty of rape." Although there was no direct connection, Whittle's grandson committed suicide. As far as African American Martinsville was concerned, anything negative happening to that family was the result of Judge Whittle's ruling in that infamous case.

Ruby Floyd left the area after the trial. Word was that she went crazy. She was already looked upon suspiciously for frequenting east Martinsville. That was an aberration because the only time a White woman could be found in our neighborhood after hours was to pick up or drop off her Black domestic worker. Ruby Floyd had been walking around door to door in the area. She was a Jehovah's Witness surrounded by a town full of rural Protestants—both Black and White. In short, after the Martinsville Seven incident, she became as much a pariah as anyone involved in the case.

Poor little Charlie Martin, who accompanied Ruby Floyd on that fateful January evening and subsequently testified at all of the Martinsville Seven trials, never got over it. In fact, Charlie was used in a way that you would never use an eleven-year-old boy in a court case today. Can you imagine the damage done to this young boy's psyche, to his spirit? He was drawn into the most infamous trial of this region, one that attracted international attention and condemnation. Apart from Ruby Floyd, Charlie Martin was the prosecution's most important witness because he placed the defendants at the scene of the attack. There was no effort to move him or his family out of the area, place him in another school, or get counseling for him. I am not aware of any direct reprisals against him, but he was shunned and avoided for most of his life. It is rumored that he, too, took to the bottle. To my knowledge, he still lives in the area.

This was one of the saddest chapters in Martinsville's history. As I said, the story continues to reverberate.

If you think that something like this can't happen today, look at the case of Brian Banks, a football player in the Los Angeles area. When he was accused of rape at sixteen, he was convicted and served six years in prison. His potential as a college player and a career in the NFL was totally derailed. In 2012, his accuser admitted no sex had taken place, as Banks had asserted all along. Fast forward to 2016 when Brock Turner, a White college swimmer at Stanford University, served only three months of a six-month sentence for sexually assaulting an intoxicated female student. With this kind of disparity between the races, this current generation's work is still not complete.

More recently, the infamous Martinsville Seven case added another chapter. In 2021, seventy-two after the trials, then-Virginia governor Ralph Northam posthumously pardoned the group, citing denial of due process rights. A few of their descendants were present for the ceremony. It was a small step to correct a horrible miscarriage of justice.

10

Aunt Marthy and Ronnie Lee

Martha Riley was, for all practical purposes, a White woman. She had blue eyes and reddish blond hair. She married Howard Riley, who may have been biracial and was rumored to have had an Italian mother. Uncle Howard had been born in New Jersey but ran away from home when he was about fifteen and worked for a time in the coal mines of West Virginia. He later moved to Henry County. Doretha thought he was handsome.

Aunt Marthy was born Martha Hairston on December 23, 1917. She was my grandfather, Jesse Ben Hairston's (Doretha's father's), younger sister and was also raised in Fieldale, Virginia, outside of Martinsville. Anyone who saw her would have thought she was Irish, Scottish, or English. Even the Black folks couldn't tell, and that was saying something, because even when White people couldn't identify someone as having Black ancestry, *we* knew. But it never dawned on African Americans that Marthy was Black.

Her father was Marshall Hairston. He looked like a little White man. He stood about 5' 2" and looked totally English, with straight hair and blue eyes. He had few, if any, African features. It was rumored that his father was Pete Hairston, the owner of the Beaver Creek Plantation.

Aunt Marthy's mother, Fannie Hairston, also had a light complexion. She had been born on the Beaver Creek Plantation and had served there as a maid. Although Marshall could have passed for White, he chose not to. He married Fannie Johnson, who was also of mixed-race ancestry. So, it is not a long stretch of the imagination that some of their kids would look more White than Black. Aunt Marthy was one of those.

Marthy started going to New York City to work when she was in her twenties before she married Uncle Howard. She lucked out and landed a job in the Duke Ellington Band as a dancer. She was also a talented pianist but mostly played by ear. I suspect she landed that job with the Ellington band because of her appearance. Although Marthy could have easily passed for White, she chose to identify as Black. There was no question that her light-skin privilege got her opportunities that darker-skinned Black women would not have had. She enjoyed playing swing jazz passages saying, "This is what Duke taught me." She may have worked with other bandleaders while she was in New York, but back home she'd play some mellow jazz on the piano.

Back in southwest Virginia, Aunt Marthy had to carry her birth certificate when she was in the car with her husband. Even though Uncle Howard was light brown-skinned, he was still obviously a Black man. They were routinely stopped by the police, and Howard would get pulled out of the car for riding around with a "White" woman. The police treated him roughly until Aunt Marthy explained that she was also a "Negro" and had a right to ride in the car with her husband. She then produced her birth certificate, which listed her race. After the explanation they were free to go, but they knew they could be stopped at any time.

One interesting story from the early 1960s highlighted the superficiality of skin color. For a long period, none of the factories in the Martinsville area would hire Black women to do any manufacturing. Fieldcrest, Tultex, and Bassett Walker all excluded Black women from employment other than serving as janitorial workers. This changed after the establishment of the Jobbers Pants Factory.

Knowing that she looked White, Aunt Marthy applied for and was hired as a factory worker at Fieldcrest. I believe she worked there for at least a year. She definitely worked there long enough for she and Uncle Howard to buy a new car. (This would have been just before the Civil Rights Act was signed.) Howard was so excited about the new car, he started taking his wife to and from work. When he took her in the morning, it would be dark, but when he picked her up, her co-workers could see her handsome *Black* husband. It didn't take long before this news reached upper management that Howard and Marthy were likely African American. She was summoned and questioned by one of the personnel managers. "Marthy, why didn't you tell us you was Colored?" Aunt Marthy said calmly, "You didn't ask!" She was immediately terminated. Fortunately, the Civil Rights Act was soon passed after this incident. Aunt Marthy got her job back at Fieldcrest, but not before suing the company for back pay. That's how she and Howard bought their house in Carver. They had enough money for a decent down payment. Marthy was sharp and knew how to use her intelligence to better her family's future. That house is still there today.

Aunt Marthy's youngest child at the time was a girl, Annette, who was born in 1953, the same as my sister Christine. She had blond curly locks like Shirley Temple with bright green eyes. I only vaguely remember her. She tragically died in 1957.

My great cousin, Patsy Riley, one of Aunt Marthy's older daughters, remembers the events surrounding her young sister's death quite well. Patsy, who was ten years old at the time, recalls the kids being outside burning leaves on a March afternoon. After the older kids went in the house, four-year-old Annette went back outside and stirred up the burning leaves with a stick. Some cinders from the burning leaves caught a hold of her clothes and set her alight. Instinctively, the little girl ran, which was the worst thing she could have done, because the oxygen only fanned the flames. Her fifteen-year-old brother ran out to help his screaming little sister. He managed to get the flaming clothes off her, but little Annette's body was badly burned. Howard and Marthy were apparently turned away from the White hospital with the explanation that their facility didn't have the capacity to handle a severe burn victim.

An emergency room physician was prepared to help the child, but after the decision about not treating her was made, the doctor followed the ambulance to Community Hospital, which catered to Black people. They were absolutely incapable of handling such a severe case. So little Annette was sent more than three hours north to Richmond's segregated Saint Philip's Hospital by ambulance. Howard and Marthy followed by car. They stayed there with their little girl until she died of pneumonia some weeks later.

For her funeral, Marthy and Howard dressed little Annette's body in white and put her in a small all-white casket. Her remains were laid to rest at Mountain Top Cemetery, and Howard and Marthy eventually placed a huge grave marker at their daughter's burial site, where it remains today. The epitaph reads, "Our little angel." Annette became yet another family member buried on that sacred ground.

* * * * * * * * * * *

Aunt Marthy had her share of family misfortunes. I was, unfortunately, drawn directly into one of these family dramas.

Uncle Howard was a tall, good-looking man. He was the color of coffee with cream in it and was a soft-spoken gentleman. His son Rudy told me he thought his daddy was part Italian, but he had no way of knowing for sure. Howard never told anyone much about his parents or childhood. Rudy said he had been mistaken for Italian in New Jersey. I tend to believe he was right. I always thought his son Howard, Jr. looked Italian.

Howard enlisted in the US Navy in 1941 before the Pearl Harbor attack but stayed in the military for several years after the war ended. For a time, he was stationed in Norfolk. When Marthy went there to visit him and they went out, some restaurants would allow her in, but not him.

Uncle Howard was a talented brick mason and taught his sons how to lay brick as well. But it was often a cyclical job, prone to periodic layoffs. When work was scarce the men would gather at their popular haunts and drink, because that was the primary social outlet for this area. This left the women to fend for their families the best way they could.

Most of the time, Uncle Howard was sugar and spice, but often those layoffs lasted for extended periods that stressed the family's finances and made things tense. So Aunt Marthy soon found herself with a house full of kids and a husband who was periodically underemployed. You would not have known anything was wrong by her expressions. Marthy eventually went to New York and worked for the Webster family. She babysat their children, although she was officially known as a "companion." In addition to sending money home, she also sent the clothes the Websters could no longer use. I believe she had all her children by then (except for the child she lost in 1957), but she kept quiet about her life in Henry County, Virginia.

As I said, Aunt Marthy easily passed for white and was, in fact, known in the area as "white" Marthy. There were two "Marthas" in Fieldale. One was called "black" Marthy who had been my Uncle Reely's fiancé, and then there was my aunt. The thing is, Aunt Marthy did not want to be identified as white. She had the opportunity to leave Henry County and live her life as a white woman. Not even black people could tell that she was not white. When she went to New York, it was to earn money and she came right back to Martinsville to take care of her husband and their chaps. When all was said and done, she loved Uncle Howard and their children. I loved her because she was so positive and encouraging. Her stories about the musicians she worked with in New York were always entertaining.

Aunt Marthy's youngest son, Ronnie Lee, was born in 1961. He was like my pretend baby when we were at church. I spoiled him. He was a beautiful little boy with dirty blond hair at the time, hazel-colored eyes, and a beautiful smile. He was darker in appearance than his mother and would not have passed for White like her. When he got a little older, I would take him out after church for a candy treat and he really loved it. He was such a sweet child, and I could see in his twinkling little eyes how much he loved me.

As Ronnie Lee grew up, however, he became more and more effeminate. I had seen those mannerisms in him when he was small but didn't pay much attention to it because it really didn't matter to me. After I left for college, he and I lost touch. I felt a little bad about letting him slip away, so I looked him up when I moved back home. When I finally located Ronnie Lee, he was wearing hot pants with small pink rollers in his hair. When I asked him what the hell was going on, he wouldn't tell me anything. It was apparent, of course, that he was a flamboyant gay man.

I had just started my job at Miller when I heard that Ronnie Lee had been beaten to a pulp by some boys in Roanoke. They blackened his eyes, busted up his lip, and cracked one of his ribs. Aunt Marthy told me about the beating, but Ronnie Lee had not given her many details. In fact, he wouldn't tell her anything, so she asked me to go see him.

When I walked into his hospital room, tears welled up in his swollen eyes when he realized it was me. I know he was embarrassed for me to see him beaten like that. His otherwise striking face was still bruised. I just sat with him without saying a word, trying to fight back my own tears. When Ronnie Lee saw tears streaming down my face, he broke down crying and said, "I'm gonna die here, Naomi." I responded, also tearfully, "Well you need to leave this area and start your life somewhere else. What about joining the army? You know the rest of your brothers have been in the military. Why don't you follow them?"

"They'd never take me."

"They wouldn't take you the way you look now, but if you cut your hair low and stop the switching, they will never suspect you're gay." He looked up at me a little stunned that I used that word to describe his obvious sexuality, but he also sensed that I was not judging him. Without dwelling on that awkward moment, Ronnie Lee responded, "Will you help me to get in?"

"Of course, I will. We better wait though, until you have healed a little more."

Some weeks later, I took him over to the local army recruiter. He still had a slightly blackened eye and a few other scrapes from the assault. Those injuries helped me to sell him as a straight kid who was just a little scrappy and needed the discipline of the military to put him on the right course. He explained to the recruiting officer how his father had been a WWII veteran, and all his brothers had since served in various branches of the military. He wanted to follow in the family tradition. Although he had dropped out of high school in the eleventh grade, Ronnie Lee was a smart boy. He did well on all the basic aptitude tests. He was admitted to the US Army and shipped off to basic training in North Carolina.

I told Aunt Marthy the military was the best thing for him, and he needed to get out of Henry County. She reluctantly nodded her head in agreement when I told her about all of this. Deep down I know she had been afraid for his safety.

Ronnie Lee kept me posted while he was in basic training, including sending me pictures of his progress. He began working out in the gym and became quite buff. He developed into a very handsome young man. I was so proud of him. I figured the army was the right move for him. Secretly, but naively, I thought he could come out of his gayness once he was away from Martinsville where kids had called him a "fag" for years. Back then, it wasn't commonly accepted that one's sexuality was genetically derived.

Ronnie Lee became an accomplished army clerk, and the military suited him so well that he re-enlisted at least twice. He had been stationed in Germany among several other places outside the country. And after his second or third re-enlistment, he was stationed at Pearl Harbor in Hawaii.

In early 1985, I received a call from Ronnie Lee inviting me to visit him at Pearl. I told him, no, I wasn't interested in going to Hawaii. About a week later he called again. This time he became persistent, almost pleading, "Naomi, please come and see me. I really need to see you." Sensing it was something urgent, I agreed to go. Before I flew out, I booked the two of us on a vacation trip to Maui, which was to depart two days after my arrival.

I flew into Oahu. The plan was for me to stay at his place near Pearl Harbor. When I arrived at the airport, I was looking around for Ronnie Lee, but didn't see him. As a result of his time in the military, he had developed a muscular frame with well-defined arms, chest, and legs. You could not miss this striking six-foot-tall handsome man, whom I was now certain was fighting women off. Because of his Cary Grant good looks, he would have certainly stood out. When I didn't see him, I became worried thinking he had been in an accident en route to meeting me.

I then heard someone calling my name very faintly, "Naomi, Naomi." When I turned in the direction of where the voice was coming from, I saw this emaciated, skin-and-bones-looking man almost hobbling towards me. It was Ronnie Lee! It was 1985 and still early in the AIDS pandemic. Ronnie Lee could tell that I was shocked by his appearance, but neither of us said anything about it. When I gave him a hug, I could feel his rib cage. That's how much weight he had lost.

As we drove back to his place, Ronnie showed me around a little. He asked me to drive his car, because he wasn't feeling well. He only told me he had developed mononucleosis. Trying to appear upbeat, I told him as I was driving, "You know we are supposed to go to Maui in two days." He said after a pause, "I really don't feel up to going to Maui. Besides, with the mono, I have a bad case of diarrhea. You go on to Maui and when you get back, hopefully I will feel better."

Ronnie Lee lived in an efficiency apartment and was going to give me his bed, but I insisted that he stay in his bed and I would use the sleeping bag. I went to Maui and had a blast, but that's when it dawned on me that Ronnie Lee had AIDS. When I returned from Maui, I was a little apprehensive about being around him, but those thoughts didn't linger long. This was the little boy that I had "mothered" when he was a baby and had looked after as a child. Also, I had known even then that the virus could not be spread through casual contact. I had seen a female interviewer kiss an HIV-infected girl on television, so I wasn't worried for my safety.

I stood on the balcony of Ronnie Lee's apartment and noticed three rainbows in the sky. I have discovered over the years not to look someone in the eyes if you really want them to tell you the truth. They will freeze up, because they don't want to see the disappointment in your face, especially if it's bad news. While looking at those rainbows with my back to Ronnie Lee, I asked, "Ronnie, do you have AIDS?" Almost as if he knew this conversation was coming, he responded, "I'm supposed to find out this evening. Will you go with me to my doctor's appointment?"

"That's why you called me out here, isn't it?" I said, still not looking in his direction.

"Yes, it is. Will you come with me, please?"

"Of course." Somehow, I felt like I was back with that little boy I had loved when he was a young child.

Ronnie Lee and I went to his medical appointment, where the doctor who had drawn his blood the previous week confirmed that he had the virus. Ronnie Lee introduced me as his sister from Martinsville, Virginia. The doctor elaborated a little about the virus and spoke to me about various precautions to be aware of. He handed me several pamphlets about HIV and AIDS, but they were very generic. When Ronnie Lee asked him how long he had to live, I stood up with the intention of leaving the room, because I didn't want to hear the doctor's response. But Ronnie Lee grabbed my arm, stopped me, and insisted that I stay. He told Ronnie Lee that based on his CD4[1] count, it was

---

[1] CD4 are so-called helper cells that fight off infections. The HIV virus kills off these cells weakening the infected person's ability to fight off the virus.

not likely he would live longer than a year, but that was not conclusive. There was no reaction from either of us to what the doctor said. We both had already suspected what was coming. I thanked the doctor for his attention to this situation and gave him my business card with my home number on it. I asked him to contact me if Ronnie Lee's condition worsened.

The drive back to Ronnie Lee's apartment was very quiet. Given the gravity of the situation, there was not much that needed to be said. For the next seven days that I was in Hawaii, however, Ronnie Lee begged me not to tell Aunt Marthy or anyone else about his health status.

> "If you tell Momma, how is it gonna' save any-
> thing? She would just be upset. I already got
> a death sentence. I'm gonna' die. Telling her
> will only make her miserable for six months,
> because that's probably all the time I have to
> live. Let me tell her when *I'm* ready."

Ronnie Lee pledged to tell his mother as time drew closer to his death, so I kept quiet and honored his request. I left Hawaii, both angry and dejected.

When I got back to Martinsville, I hadn't properly landed before Aunt Marthy sought me out. "How's my Ronnie Lee? I am so proud of him. I know he wouldn't have been over there had it not been for you, 'cause you're one of the best things that's ever happen' to this family." I glanced in her direction but couldn't look at her eye to eye. I was afraid she would suspect something. I wanted to tell her what had happened, but I had promised Ronnie Lee. I often wondered if she knew I was holding something back from her.

In addition to leaving all his military benefits to his mother, Ronnie Lee had taken out a life insurance policy on himself so that when he died, Aunt Marthy would have money to bury him with a healthy amount left over for her personal use.

When he died, Ronnie Lee's remains were brought back to Martinsville. This was supposedly the first time someone with AIDS had been funeralized in the town. Hairston's Funeral Home placed a net over his open casket because even in death, some felt the virus was contagious.

Before he died, Ronnie Lee asked that I speak at his funeral. I did, but it just about tore me to pieces. I told those in attendance about the little boy I once held and what a special and happy child he had been. I also told them about the man and the soldier he had become. I explained how he had followed in the proud footsteps of his father and brothers in defending our country. I also spoke about his Cary Grant good looks but made no mention of his sexual orientation. It wasn't the place for any of that.

As Aunt Marthy was presented with the American flag that had been draped over Ronnie Lee's casket at the gravesite, she fainted. Marthy had now buried two children. Ronnie Lee's sexuality had been a disappointment to Marthy, but she never judged him. Howard, Marthy, and his brothers and sisters had every reason to be proud of his honorable service in the U.S. military. Had Ronnie Lee been in the military now, he would have had a very different experience. Fortunately, we have moved beyond such discriminatory practices in the country's fighting forces, at least on paper.

When I said earlier I was angry when I left Ronnie Lee in Hawaii, there was a reason. He had bared his soul to me about everything. He told me he had been molested as a child by a neighbor. Ronnie Lee said he could not remember a time when that man had not sodomized him as a boy. When he was about five, he remembered this neighbor penetrating him with his finger. Ronnie Lee believed that inappropriate touching is what made him the way he was. Add to that, he thought his daddy, Uncle Howard, didn't like him because he was not like his brothers.

When Ronnie Lee was at Carver High School, he opened up to a guidance counselor about the sexual abuse he had been subjected to. Not only did he tell the counselor about his next-door neighbor, but also about the other sexual liaisons he had had with several well-placed Black men in Henry County, including a medical practitioner and other high school officials. Instead of the guidance counselor reporting that these "respected" men had been having sex with a fourteen-year-old boy to his mother, the counselor sat and listened to this boy describe these "relationships." Ronnie Lee told me the counselor even asked him for the specifics of what kind of sex had taken place between him and these men as if the counselor was titillated by this debauchery. I was fuming with outrage at that guidance counselor for neglecting this boy.

The counselor was just as guilty as those men who had abused Ronnie Lee. At the very least, the counselor was culpable. I even wondered for a time if the counselor had used that information to extort things from those men. The counselor could have at least gone to them and said that they knew about the men's down-low sexual activities with a minor as a means of stopping this abuse. Even if the counselor didn't want him to go to the authorities, it would have been better than doing nothing. It's not likely anything would have happened to those men in a small town like Martinsville at the time, but these days such actions would have been punishable by imprisonment.

Instead, the counselor encouraged Ronnie Lee to keep his abuse a secret. That's part of our Southern culture—you keep these filthy activities quiet. So there I was in paradise being told things about my idyllic Martinsville that could have curled most people's hair. And that's how my precious little Ronnie Lee grew up in Henry County, Virginia.

He was obviously very bitter over the course of that week I was with him. He was especially angry about dying. Ronnie Lee said, "I don't care who I have sex with now and I'm not wearin' a condom. Somebody gave this thing to me and I'm gon' give it to anybody who has sex with me. I don't give a damn!"

"Ronnie, that's wrong," I said.

"I don't give a shit. And don't lecture me. If somebody wants to have sex with me, I'll tell 'em, 'Come on.'"

He also told me that years earlier when he had been beaten up in Roanoke, he had been having sex with one of his assailants. But when it started to get around that the boy he had been having sex with was also gay, the boy and some of his friends attacked Ronnie Lee in order to prove the boy's masculinity. Even in his emaciated condition, Ronnie was still an attractive young man. I prayed that he didn't carry through with his threat to spread that virus.

When he finally told Aunt Marthy about his illness, she was devastated. He told her about a month before he died. He passed away at an army hospital in Georgia on July 9, 1986. Aunt Marthy was not the same after that, but she never said a word to me on the subject. She was almost resigned to the fact that she would follow her baby boy to the grave. As it happened, however, Marthy lived another ten years after Ronnie Lee. Uncle Howard, on the other hand, died four months to the day after his youngest son. Uncle Howard, Aunt Marthy, and Ronnie Lee are all buried near each other at Carver Memorial Gardens where so many other family members are now at rest.

11

William B. Muse, Jr.

*T*here were times when I thought I would never get married. I had so many responsibilities surrounding Koehler Hollow and keeping this family functioning, which included raising Doretha's children. But I was fortunate to marry a wonderful man, even though he was significantly older.

My husband, William Brown Muse, Jr., was born July 7, 1918, which happened to be the same birth date and year as the late South African icon, Nelson Mandela. Bill Muse was the second of six children and the firstborn son in the family. Bill's story is significant as it represents a life far more privileged than mine. Yet, it's still very much a part of the African American Appalachian experience.

After returning to Koehler Hollow when I graduated from Virginia Union in 1975, I spent twenty years bringing my family's homestead into the twentieth century. At the time we had no indoor plumbing or running water. It was a textbook definition of poverty. I had the means, so I felt obliged to help those who had nurtured and raised me. I did what Doretha should have done for her family but couldn't because of economic constraints.

I neglected to get married and didn't even date that often during those years. I primarily worked at Miller Brewing Company and farmed. In addition to installing plumbing, I added bedrooms onto the house and cleared off more of the property for agricultural purposes. Then, I moved back to Koehler and started raising animals. I was on a schedule at Miller where I worked three or four days and was off the rest. It was wonderful. I absolutely loved it. I had twenty goats, ten pigs, chickens, turkeys, and a Black Angus cow, among other animals. I loved farming. I milked my goats and pasteurized the milk.

In 1987, I went to a party and my late mentor, Dr. Valley W. Hylton, was there. He was speaking to a rather distinguished-looking elderly man. He invited me over and asked, "Naomi, are you married?

"No, sir."

"Are you dating anyone?"

"No, sir." I was a little taken aback by such a forward question.

"Well, I have the perfect man for you." He was speaking about Bill Muse, which is how he and I met. I thought to myself, "This man is old enough to be my daddy." Bill and I talked that evening. He was polite enough, but it was mostly small talk. As it turned out, I had just begun learning how to play golf. I had borrowed some clubs from a colleague at work. Bill, as fate had it, turned out to be an avid golfer and said, "I'll teach you how to play." We played golf for months and that progressed to going out to dinner. Suddenly, we were boyfriend and girlfriend. It was not planned, but I have to say he was quite intriguing.

William Brown Muse, Jr. was born in Danville, Virginia, and all his siblings were born there. The family had moved there from Franklin County. Bill's father and grandfather had been personal friends of Booker T. Washington. The Muses had a huge farm in Penhook, Virginia. Muse family lore held that Bill's great-grandfather, a White planter, was named Frankie Muse.[1] After Frankie Muse's death, William Brown Muse, Sr., inherited the land from his father. William B. Muse, Sr., eventually relocated to Danville and worked as a railroad postal clerk. He processed the mail on the train. His job required him to travel as well.[2]

In 1928, there was a train robbery that made the papers throughout the region. Several bags of cash were discovered missing from the train's money car. The Pullman porters eventually came under suspicion because they had access to the car where the money had been stored. Bill Muse, Sr., happened

---

[1] The veteran African American Civil Rights attorney and 2011 NAACP Spingarn winner, Frankie Muse Freeman (1916–2018), was named after this forbear. Her autobiography, *A Song of Faith and Hope: The Life of Frankie Muse Freeman* was helpful in parts of this chapter.

[2] Freeman, Frankie Muse, *A Song of Faith and Hope*, p. 7

to not be working the day of the robbery, so he was not under suspicion. The robbery was under investigation for months before a lead was found.

Someone at a bus stop in Danville was overheard talking about one of the Pullman porters who had been working on the day of the robbery. It seems this particular porter had painted one room of his house yellow and another blue. Back then, white paint was all any Black family could afford. Having different color paints was so unheard of that it was suspicious. In any case, the conversation was reported to the railroad authorities, and the local constable believed that this had somehow been connected to the train robbery from a few months earlier. All three of the Pullman porters working the day of the robbery were arrested and charged. All of them lived in the Danville area.

When the case went to trial, the porters were represented by the Black law firm Williams, Luck, and Williams, also based in Danville. The prosecuting and defense attorneys decided on a bench trial, which left it to the judge to decide the guilt or innocence of the porters. When the trial got underway, the prosecutor alleged that the three porters had conspired to steal the money bags and over the subsequent months had spent parts of the money on things like paints and other luxury items. When the defense attorney objected and asked the prosecutor to identify the luxury items purchased to substantiate the monetary windfall, the prosecution's witness cited the porter who had painted rooms in his house different colors. The judge was not impressed. The prosecutor continued laying out his case that the Pullman porters had thrown the money bags off the train in an agreed-upon location and, with an unnamed accomplice, absconded with the money. The prosecutor argued that the train robbery had taken detailed planning, precision, sophistication, and daring to execute. As the prosecutor brought in technical experts to demonstrate how the robbery had been staged, the defense attorney never raised an objection.

When it was time to put on his case, the defense attorney reiterated the prosecutor's argument about the careful, meticulous, complex nature of the robbery. Then, he addressed the judge directly. "Y'honor, look at these 'niggas.' Just look at these poor dumb 'niggas!' Do they look like they are smart enough to pull off a sophisticated robbery like this and get away with all that money? I mean, y'honor, really? Even if they had, do you think they're smart enough not to have spent any of it up by now?"

Before the trial got underway, the defense attorney had instructed his clients to hang their heads, not comb their hair, and look as pitiful and forlorn as possible, which they did. Given the racial stereotypes of southwest Virginia in the 1920s, the judge seemed to have bought into the defense's "ignorant black man" strategy. After all, could these intellectually inferior men pull off such a technically sophisticated robbery? The judge acquitted the three Pullman porters for lack of evidence.

The story doesn't end there. William B. Muse, Sr., sent all six of his children to universities like Hampton and Shaw. Each one had a new car when they left for college, and all completed their educations with no debt. Remember that when those money bags were thrown off the train, someone had to pick them up and William Muse, Sr., was not at work that day. Bill's face would turn cherry red when he told me that story and that's all he'd say about the train robbery.

* * * * * * * * * * *

Bill was drafted into the U.S. Army after Pearl Harbor was attacked. Some of his White relatives pulled strings and got him assigned as a warrant officer, so he never saw any combat. He had recently married his first wife, Evelyn, who he met while they were students at Hampton Institute.

When Bill returned to southwest Virginia from WWII, Black men were not allowed to build safe and sanitary housing (which simply meant housing with indoor plumbing). He knew the Servicemen's Readjustment Act of 1944 (the GI Bill) was also available to Black veterans. Bill wanted nothing more than to enlarge his business interests and build appropriate housing for African Americans in Martinsville. He did not realize, however, the depth of the racism he would confront. The local banks worked with White GIs to finance homes but refused Black veterans the same rights. So African Americans were relegated to living in shacks with outhouses. It didn't matter if you had been a soldier and qualified for a GI loan. The banks just wouldn't give them to us.

This racism wasn't just applied to soldiers. As a Black physician, Dr. Williams obviously had the financial wherewithal to pay the bank, but was also denied a mortgage loan. When he attempted to borrow $23,000, he was told by the bank officer, "What Colored person could buy a $23,000 house if you were to default on this loan? We wouldn't be able to sell the house, because of the location" (i.e., in a segregated Black neighborhood.). He had to go to North Carolina Mutual, a Black insurance company that provided housing loans, to finance his house.

The banks took the position that a home with a bathroom was too expensive for Black people. Bill became more resolved than ever to "provide safe and sanitary housing to people of color," which was his company's motto. To that end, he ran the financing through North Carolina Mutual for the housing he built and sold.

"Honey," my nickname for Bill, broke the mold. Against his father's wishes, he did not major in education, but in business and accounting. Bill never intended to work for anyone but himself. He established real estate companies in Danville and Martinsville and his first wife, Evelyn, ran them while he served in World War II. She also operated his insurance company and other businesses when he needed help. Bill and Evelyn had three sons, Billy, Michael, and Eric, all of whom were college-educated men. Yet, tragedy struck when Evelyn Muse received a cancer diagnosis and died in 1979. He never thought he would recover from her death. He later told me, "I was a millionaire for a brief period and then Evelyn took ill."

An area bank, Imperial Savings and Loan, had been established in Martinsville in January 1929. By the mid-1940s, after Honey returned from the war, Imperial was functionally insolvent. The original owner, Mr. Spencer, had done his best, but he was ready to retire and the institution had a negative value of $100,000. To bail the bank out, Honey and three of his closest friends put up $25,000 each—the minimum amount required to stop the savings and loan from defaulting. Once again, Bill turned over the day-to-day operations of his other businesses to Evelyn, while he put all his effort into rebuilding Imperial Savings and Loan.

Receiving protection from the federal savings and loan insurance system seemed out of reach for Imperial until a friend told Bill of a White House maid, who agreed to approach President Nixon on his behalf. Sure enough, the maid asked the president about the matter and he agreed to have someone investigate it. The call from the White House opened the door for Imperial to become a member of The Federal Deposit Insurance Corporation (FDIC).

Bill mentored many African Americans on how to get into housing. He had a very relevant quote, "If you can't afford to get in it [a house], you won't be able to stay in it." Even today, people tell me how Honey helped them to get houses or inherited homes he financed from their parents or other family members. But as committed as he was, Bill had his detractors. Anytime someone is involved in real estate and property rentals, there will inevitably be those who don't pay up. When it was necessary, he evicted people. And several of them held grudges against him. It was Evelyn who handled these matters, but Bill Muse's name was on the properties, and the evictees held him accountable.

Bill's reputation grew as he worked with Imperial Savings and Loan, as did his involvement with the NAACP and the Henry County's Voters League. Bill came to know Poppa because of their mutual interest in registering Black people to vote in Henry County. They wouldn't have otherwise crossed paths as they belonged to different social classes. Bill was the local NAACP president in the late 1940s and 50s during the height of the Martinsville Seven incident and remained in that position for years. He served again in the 1990s, and I attended those meetings with him. He was still working full-time. When his health began to decline, he cut back on those activities. The local NAACP chapter eventually dissolved.

Imperial Savings and Loan became the backbone for bailing out civil rights arrestees. When there was Black civil disobedience for protesting in front of Woolworths, Green's, or Globman's, the bank put up the bail money. Bill also founded a men's group known as the Men's Round Table in the 1960s, which was an organization that provided mentoring and kept the Black community informed on various laws affecting them and their rights. That organization folded in the 1970s when it refused to allow women as participants.

Another of Bill's political goals was to place two African Americans on the Martinsville City Council. He succeeded in getting one person on the council. It took a few more years before others continued his work to get a second African American elected.

Bill also became active in the Virginia Democratic Party. He helped to raise money for candidates, mentored some on how to appeal to Blacks and Whites in this part of the state, and organized small and large campaign meetings. That led to his association with former Governor L. Douglas Wilder, whom he supported for lieutenant governor and then governor of Virginia. Bill continued to serve as president of the bank until he retired in 1991.

When he and I met in 1987, he had been alone for some years. We dated for two years before marrying at his house on First Street in 1989. We were married by a Ugandan Episcopal bishop who was an exile in the United States after being implicated in an uprising in his country. It was a small wedding. Grandma Dollie, Doretha, and my friends Darlene and Pat were my witnesses and attendants.

Bill loved my nieces and nephews, especially Christine's son Paul. He called him "Little Colonel." Paul loved him as well. When he got married, Paul said, "I want to be a husband just like Uncle Bill. He has shown me what a husband ought to be." Honey was also devoted to his grandchildren.

In 2004, my darling Bill began having a series of transient ischemic attacks, or small strokes. He was well into his eighties by then. Even though he was weakened by these episodes, he was able to handle his affairs. Because I was still fully employed at Miller, I hired a home health service to assist us. Doretha (who was living with us by then) also helped him out when I was at work. She drove him around and assisted him with other tasks. Later that year, he had a significant health event and had to be hospitalized. I could hear his labored breathing, which I could tell was fluid on his lungs. We used to call that kind of breathing "chain-stoking." Some people called it the "death rattle."

Our primary care doctor told me Bill had lived a long life and I should "let him go." I was stunned. When I realized what he'd meant, I fired him on the spot. I spoke to another physician about bringing in a respiratory therapist to take over. After that specialist came in, they pulled the phlegm off Honey's lungs. Within a few hours, he sat up and ate his dinner.

Despite his recovery from the lung problem, Bill was not able to come back home after the hospital stay and I had to put him in an extended-care facility in 2005. Later in the year, Jesse Ben Hodge, my birth father, reemerged and his brief stay stretched my budget to the breaking point. Bill began to develop dementia, but I kept him immaculately dressed in the facility. I made sure he always had a week's worth of washed and pressed clothing. I took him to church every Sunday. The facility had him dressed neatly in his suit every weekend. After church, we went to eat fried chicken, which he loved. I always kept a bowl of cookies and candy beside his bed at the facility for the staff who attended to him. On holidays, I made sure they had a special treat.

On February 28, 2007, Honey passed away. William B. Muse, Jr., was laid to rest on March 3, 2007, next to his mother and father in Danville. I'd never felt so lonely in my entire life as I did after he died. Although it has been seventeen years, I still miss him. Grandma Dollie quoted Alfred Lord Tennyson's famous line, "T'is better to have loved and lost, than never to have loved at all." That summarizes my time with Bill Muse. Despite our age difference, he was a wonderful husband and partner.

In the early 2000s, there was a movement to revive the Martinsville chapter of the NAACP. A local minister spearheaded the revival, but that didn't last very long. In 2005, I finally became a life member. In 2008, I became the regional director for Barack Obama's presidential campaign. I encouraged a local businessman, Tony Milner, to run for president of the local NAACP, and he won. I was elected as vice-president. When Tony took over the leadership, we had less than a dollar in the organizational account, so out of his pocket, he paid the fees to make the chapter solvent with the national organization. I was elected NAACP president in 2010 and am currently serving my eighth term.

12

Uncle Jordan

*U*ncle Jordan was related to us on Momma Rosie's side of the family. He served in World War I. When Uncle Jordan was a young man during the Great Depression, he had to change trains in a West Virginia town that was notorious for killing Black men and boys. The train arrived there around 1:00 AM, and he got off. The train he needed to transfer to came an hour or two later.

Uncle Jordan made sure he stayed close to the train station because he didn't want any trouble. He had heard about the town's reputation. As he told me, "Lo and behold, three White men came up to me and said, 'Nigger, you gon' die dis night.'" He said they didn't know who the hell they were messing with. Uncle Jordan said,

> "I had my .38 caliber with me, and my hand was
> on it. When they made a step towards me, I gut-
> shot every last one of 'em. I dropped 'em dead.
> I dragged their bodies behind the station. When
> the train came back by, I got on it. I was the only
> person gettin' dat train. Dem sons of bitches
> thought they were gon' kill me in the middle of
> the night. They don' los' 'd'eir minds."

I was young when Uncle Jordan first told me this story. As I got a little older, I came to believe he was exaggerating until my stepdaddy Pokechop told me a similar story with a different ending. He went through the same West Virginia town, and it was also early in the morning when he got there. He got off the train and the man at the window told him,

> "Boy, you don't need to stand 'round here
> 'cause there's some bad men here and they will
> kill you. I need you to go over there and get
> in that drainage tube and hide. Your train ain't
> comin' till 6:00 PM. Now don't you come out.
> I'll bring you some lunch, but you stay in that
> pipe. When the train gets here, you wait until
> that train is 'bout ready to take off and you
> make a beeline and jump on it. I tell you I seen
> some bad things take place here to your kind."

And so Pokechop did like the railroad clerk told him. He sat in that huge drainage pipe the whole day. Sure to his word, the clerk brought him lunch. Right around 6:00 PM, the clerk came and banged loudly on the pipe. Pokechop sprang out as instructed and ran for the train as if he were running for his life. He literally was doing just that. Some of the people in the station thought he was running from someone, but there was no one behind him giving chase. He made it on the train, tipped his hat to the clerk in the station, and took his seat. Years later, I saw a PBS special about that West Virginia town and how it was notorious for killing Black men. Having heard this story from two different sources about the same town, I became a believer.

* * * * * * * * * *

As a child I thought Uncle Jordan was a real cowboy. He was like a living John Wayne or Matt Dillon. I remember all the magical and surreal tales he told. He was an avid storyteller who always painted a picture as he spoke.

Jordan Mars (Martin) was born in Franklin County. He was the son of one of Momma Rosie's sisters. Uncle Jordan was an extremely handsome, yet very unstable, man. He stood about six-foot-two with wide shoulders and had a reddish-brown complexion. He had poker-straight hair. Jordan always wore a Stetson hat and a bolo tie. When he got dressed up, he was the prettiest thing I'd ever seen. He took me fishing when I was young and that's when he told me several of these incredible life stories.

Part of the reason why I have so many of these stories to tell is that I listened to the old folks in our family, and it often made my day to hear them. It was a magical time. I've always loved hearing these stories and developed a love of telling stories. People in our family often recounted these family adventures, but many times young people weren't willing to listen, so the stories were lost. The following Uncle Jordan story took place in the early 1920s.

He told me, "I used to make me some liquor. I mean I *made* some liquor! I had me a still up in Franklin County, and I was a rich man." Back then, if you went to jail, you lost the rights to your military pension. Uncle Jordan said, "I was bootleggin' and makin' fine money. I had $20,000 in the bank. Who heard of a Colored man with $20,000? I married this pretty little yella gal. She was 'bout as pretty a thing as you ever wanted to see in your life. Had hair all the way down to her hind end. And it was poker straight. Once a little birdie told me there was a white man who drove a yella cab was comin' to my house cuttin' my time [i.e., having an affair with his wife].

> "I decided I was gon' go out of Rocky Mountains [in Franklin County] and was gon' to find out whether dat cab driver was at my house. I came home unannounced on a Saturday night at 3:00 in the mornin'. Sure enough, there was

a yella cab parked upside my house. I crept in the house and don't cha know dat White man was on top of my wife humpin' away. It made me so mad, I reckon I grab me a hand full of his hair, yanked back his head, and *slit* his throat. When I yanked his head back, my wife saw me, screamed, and jumped out the bedroom window, buck naked, and took off. She was as naked as a jaybird, but she ran. I went to the window to go after her, but I was too big to fit through the window. I had to run back through the house and go out the front door. I ran as fast as I could 'cause I was gon' cut her throat too, but she was too fast for me. I was still mad as hell, so I went back home and dat summa bitch White man was naked layin' over in the bedroom corner gurglin'. I pulled his head back again and said, 'You ain't dead yet?' And I cut his throat some more.

Well, dey put me in jail for it. You know dat summa bitch didn't die, but it won't for lack of effort, 'cause I surely did try. Luck just had it, dat fool didn't see his maker dat day. But he was deformed for the rest of his life. He walked with his head hung over to the left side. I must've cut some lig'ments in his neck, 'cause he couldn't hold his head up straight or

talk right after dat night. I told 'em you won't
be messin' around with nobody else's wife.
You know, I couldn't see dem puttin' me in
jail for dat. I mean me catchin' another man on
top of my wife like dat. After dem White folks
got every penny of my $20,000 savings, dey
still give me twenty years. Dey sent me up to
500 Spring Street in Richmond.[1]

Dem Paddy rollers beat nigga's assess with
big black leather paddles. Dey would jes' beat'
chu for nothin'. Dey would bend you over a
barrel and beat' chu! One of the jobs dey gave
me was to put fifty-pound sand bags on the
men dey don' 'lectrocuted to straightin' 'em
out so dey could put 'em in a box to bury. When
dey 'lectrocuted 'em, dey'd be froze and we'd
have to break 'em back in shape. I guess I had
been at 500 Spring Street about five years and
had a reputation for speakin' up to the guards.
Dese five inmates came to me and said, 'We
gon' break out this place. We got ourselves a
plan.' I said, 'Okay, I'm wit' you boys.' But the

---

[1] This is the address of the former Virginia State Penitentiary in
Richmond. It was built in the 19th century before the Civil War and
closed in 1990. The facility was condemned by the ACLU as the
"most shameful prison in America." Those who lived inside called it
"The Wall."

more I listened to dem 'splain things to me, I thought to myself, 'These niggas gon' get dey asses killed.' I then thought to myself, 'Maybe I can get somethin' out of this.' When I got the chance, I told the old sergeant I needed to see the warden. When I got to him, I said, 'Cap'an' I know some boys in here who gon' try to break out.' I just told it. The warden told me to just play along and act like nothin' had happened. I was to make 'em believe I was still workin' wit' 'em, and I did just dat. When it came time for 'em to make their move, I hung back. The warden's men shot 'em all down—all five of 'em. Dey just shot 'em down like dogs. To reward me for co-operatin', the warden reduced my sentence. I was sent up to Spencer[2] to the work release camp to serve the balance of my time."

That's how Uncle Jordan got out of prison—by ratting out these other Black guys and getting them killed. His sentence was significantly reduced. He figured they were going to get killed anyway, so he might as well get something out of it. That's how cold he could be.

---

[2] A low security facility in Henry County.

* * * * * * * * * * *

Once I was babysitting some kids at the Hollow and I decided to go down the hill to visit Uncle Jordan. He sat there with us on his porch. He had a beautiful mimosa tree in his yard. It bloomed in the spring with pink buds and little fine green leaves.

Uncle Jordan was not in one of his best moods that day. A branch of the mimosa tree hung over the porch near where we stood. Out of nowhere, Uncle Jordan said, "I'm tired of that damn tree limb." The next thing you know he took up his shotgun, aimed upwards, and boom. He blew the limb off the tree, and it came down on the top of our heads with a big swoosh! Doretha came screaming and hollering to see what was wrong. I was so used to Uncle Jordan that it didn't even upset me. He scared the daylights out of those kids I was babysitting, though.

Uncle Jordan was so mean he once had me go to the store and buy him an extension cord. Once he got it, he peeled the plastic off the cord, exposing the bare wire. He ran it around the tree and plugged it in. When a dog came to heist his leg to pee on the tree, it would get the shock of its life. He was just straight-out mean.

He and I would go fishing when I was a little girl of about nine or ten. Uncle Jordan would stop at the store down in Koehler and buy a six-pack of Country Club Malt Liquor. He'd buy me a Nehi soda and a bag of Cheetos. That Nehi was strong. We'd fish all day behind the banks of the block plant. After Uncle Jordan got drunk, he'd reach in his pocket, pull out his gun, and shoot in the river—bam, bam, bam, bam! He'd call out his familiar dictum: "I'm half black, half Indian, and all crazy!" He'd shoot off his gun some more. I loved it. I never told Doretha or Grandma Dollie what Uncle Jordan did, because if I had they wouldn't let me go fishing with him and that could not happen.

Sometime later he and I were down near Heights Oil Company sitting on a huge root of a sycamore tree that grew right over the top of the river. Appalachian Power let the water out at twelve noon, which caused the river to rise, and it would stay up. Uncle Jordan was telling some of his far-flung stories about his exploits.

He told me about when he went down to Mexico (which he pronounced may-he-ko) and married him one of them "Carmelitas." He said, "There are some pretty women down there." He then showed me a scar on his arm. It was about six to eight inches long. It went from one side to the other. He continued,

> "Gal, I was down in 'Mayheko.' I had two chaps
> down there. Some of dem Mexicans can be real
> nice and dark like Colored folks and Indians.
> My wife down there was real jealous. I didn't
> do no beatin' or knockin' on her, because she
> had some real mean brothers. Anyway, I was
> in one of dem cantinas and d'is other pretty
> little 'Carmelita' come and starts talkin' to me.

I leaned my arm up against the wall 'cause she was short. Don't cha know my wife ran over and stabbed me in my arm and it stuck to the damn wall. Den she commenced ta cryin'. *I* was the one in pain. If anybody should'a been cryin', it should'a been me. After a minute, my wife pulled dat knife out and dressed the wound real nice, still cryin' as she was fixin' on me. We made up 'cause she just cried and cried. I finally said, 'Honey, I forgive you,' but I thought ta myself, 'Like hell I will.' I waited til' she went ta sleep. The baby started cryin' I got up and put a bottle in his mouth and come the hell up out of Mayheko and ain't never went back."

Uncle Jordan said that was the only woman who didn't run away because he ran away from her. I asked him about his chaps down in Mexico. Wasn't he curious about what happened to them? He just looked at me and shrugged his shoulders. That was Uncle Jordan.

* * * * * * * * * *

I used to enjoy watching *Wrestling from Roanoke* on WDBJ 7 television in the early 1960s. That was long before the WWE and Rick Flair. The program came on at 1:00 PM on Saturdays. It became a family favorite. One day I went down to Uncle

Jordan's to watch a big wrestling match. He sat in his house all day long with a shotgun across his lap. Don't ask me why, but that's just how he did. I think he kept it like that just in case he had to shoot somebody who caught up with him from his past.

Anyway, we were sitting there watching the wrestling match. Sailor Art Thomas, one of the few African American celebrity wrestlers, had come into the ring. He typically stood in the middle of the ring and made his pecs jump up and down. He was a hero among the Black people of the area, and Uncle Jordan's favorite wrestler. Another one of Jordan's favorites was Sweet Daddy Siki. He was a more colorful character than Sailor Art Thomas. Sweet Daddy eventually dyed his hair blond and married a White woman. That invited the attention of the Ku Klux Klan throughout many Southern venues where he wrestled.

One Saturday, Sailor Art Thomas was wrestling George Oleander. I think it must have been a tag team match where two wrestlers teamed up against two opposing wrestlers. There were few rules in these matches, so it was possible to have a two-against-one scenario if one of the wrestlers was down. One wrestler jumped Sailor. He hit him in his manly parts pretty bad. Both wrestlers jumped in his stomach, and he rolled over writhing in pain. He nearly passed out.

Uncle Jordan was outraged and said, "Dem some dirty sons of bitches." He pointed his shotgun at the TV set and pulled the trigger—boom! I watched the television explode. Once he calmed down, Jordan looked at me with my eyes still wide open and said, "Gal, go up to the house and call me a cab. I'ma have to buy me a new TV set." It was your average day with Uncle Jordan. He never let up.

* * * * * * * * * * *

Growing up in the woods, we were away from everybody. The outside world stopped on the other side of our mailbox. It was like being in our very own universe.

Wootsie and Uncle Jordan both had a fondness for bootleg liquor and they both drank too much. Being from the country, it seemed like everybody was a crack shot with a pistol or a shotgun. Even Momma Rosie, who was as gentle a woman you were ever likely to know, was a good shot. She could hit anything with her pistol. Poppa had a shotgun and a German Luger. After Poppa died, Wootsie used Poppa's gun and Uncle Jordan had a double-barrelled shotgun.

One day, Wootsie and Uncle Jordan were "woofin'" at each other about who was the better shot. Uncle Jordan told Wootsie he could shoot his shotgun as fast as she could pull the trigger on that German Luger that had once belonged to Poppa. I was invited to be the spotter, which meant I told them when to commence shooting their respective weapons. Wootsie got her automatic pistol. All you needed to do was pull the trigger. It looked like a .45, but it was bigger. Uncle Jordan put the shells between his fingers—one, two, three. His barrel was cocked and fully loaded.

On the count of three I told them both to shoot—not at each other, but down the hill toward the woods at a target that I had identified for them. When I gave the signal to shoot Wootsie came up with her pistol and it went bam, bam, bam, bam, bam, bam! Uncle Jordan's gun was even louder—boom, boom, crack, boom, boooom! It was totally awesome! The contest was a tie! Uncle Jordan came up with a double-barrelled shotgun, shot those two shells, flocked that gun down, threw two more shells in it, and came back up and shot again. His speed was amazing. You talk about country—that was real country. It was a glorious day in the Hollow.

Uncle Jordan got a leukemia diagnosis in his later life. His cancer went into remission at one point but had come back by 1982. One Sunday, he waited for his daughter to go to church, put a gun in his mouth, and pulled the trigger. It was almost poetic that he chose to go out like this. After the trauma of his suicide had passed, I realized that Jordan had ended his life on his own terms. And did it as dramatically and violently as he had lived his life.

One of my deepest regrets, however, was not persuading Uncle Jordan to get saved. He had lived a life of violence, mayhem, and debauchery, but he never stole. Uncle Jordan said he was married five times and never once got a divorce. Doretha didn't like me to be around him because she thought he was a bad influence. That never stopped me from seeing him though.

13

Cody

This narrative of events took place in and around my Koehler Hollow experience. Many of those experiences were positive, but this story clearly falls into a different category. It's a difficult story to tell—parts of it are quite painful. But it was as much a part of living in the Hollow as the good stories.

Cody Landon (not his real name) stood about six feet two inches tall and was extremely thin. I have no idea of when or how he and Doretha met, but when it came to attracting dysfunctional relationships, Doretha was a pro. I honestly believe the more dangerous they were, the more she was drawn to them. Add to that, Cody was also ten years Doretha's junior.

When he was a teenager, Cody lost his right ear in a car accident and had to wear a plastic prosthetic. He also had a pronounced scar on that side of his face that ran from his ear down to his mouth. He had played basketball for Carver High

School, and he also drank excessively. One night after a game, he was carousing with his friends and was in a terrible car wreck in which most of his ear was cut off. The White doctor who treated him in the ER saw his ear hanging by a piece of skin off the side of his head and just jerked the ear off and threw it in the trash. After the loss of his right ear, Cody's balance was compromised, so he had to abandon his ambitions to play college basketball.

As wicked as he was, Cody had not come from a bad family. In fact, his father, Mr. Landon, was a very good man. He was a salt-of-the-earth kind of person. He owned a successful taxi service and was kind enough to let people pay him on their time when they couldn't afford it. After I won a local 4-H public speaking contest, Mr. Landon came to Koehler to give me a ride to town to catch the bus to the regional competition. It was in the early stages of integration, and I was the first Black person to compete against the White kids. I was told to be at the courthouse in downtown Martinsville for a 6:00 AM departure. I was so excited, I got there just after 5:30 to assure I was on time. As Mr. Landon and I pulled up in his taxi, we saw the bus pulling off. I was puzzled momentarily, but then I realized that I had been lied to about the departure time. I jumped out of the taxi and chased the bus waving my arms. I could see the White kids on the bus laughing at me. I stopped and started crying. Mr. Landon drove up to where I had stopped and said, "Stop dat cryin' right now gal. You did not a single thing wrong. Dem peckerwoods told you de wrong time on purpose." He ordered me into the car and took me back to the Hollow while I was still wiping away tears. He didn't charge Doretha a cent for taking or bringing me back. As I said, he was a real good man.

Mr. Landon's son, on the other hand, turned out to be horrid. He was an alcoholic, an abuser of women, a liar, and an out-and-out monster. He was as close to evil as I have ever known someone to be. Doretha, in one of her famously foolish decisions, became enamored with this younger man, whom I believed to be Beelzebub.

Cody had a good-paying job but spent his money on whiskey. Once he came to the Hollow with a huge bucket of Kentucky Fried Chicken. Living in the sticks, we had never tasted anything like that before. But I remember the look from him while we ate the chicken. It was a sinister smirk as if to say, "You poor dumb niggas. It only took a bucket of chicken for me to buy you." When I saw that smug look on his face, I immediately gave my chicken to Christine or David and refused to touch another piece. That was only a harbinger of what was to come.

Grandma Dollie let Cody live in a room in her house just down the hill from the main house, but Doretha didn't stay there with him while Grandma was around. He stayed drunk much of the time, and I never got used to this younger man bossing Doretha around like she was a child. I resented that the most.

As I said earlier, I would follow Grandma Dollie down the hill to her house after she had too much to drink at the main

house. I didn't want anything to happen to her as she staggered home. Once, Grandma put me in her bed and lay beside
me for a while as usual. It was her custom to get up during the
night and sit in the kitchen after I fell asleep. Cody decided to
crawl up into the bed with me after Grandma left the room. I
must have been about twelve at the time. In other words, I was
nearing adolescence. I was fast asleep when I heard Grandma
call out, "Gal, who's that in the bed with you!?" When she
said it, I couldn't quite comprehend what she meant, because
I thought I was lying next to her. I finally managed to get out,
"You are," still dozy. She said, "No, I'm not," which is when I
immediately became alert. It was Cody with his arms wrapped
around me. As I was pushing him away from me, Grandma
Dollie rushed off and got a broom to beat him. "How *dare* you
get in bed with this child!? How dare you? How dare you?"
She continued beating him with that broom even after he got
out of her bed. In fact, she beat him back into his room. It was
like she was battling some kind of monster. She stayed in that
room with me for the rest of that night. She dozed off once or
twice sitting in the chair. Once she adjusted her seated position, I could see she had been sitting on her gun.

That was the end of me going down to Grandma Dollie's
house, which really hurt me. Our treks down the hill to her
place had been a time of bonding with my grandmother.
Because of that wicked Cody, those times came to an end. I'm
sure Grandma never said anything to Doretha about Cody
and neither did I. At the time, Doretha was so enamored with

that fool, she would have excused it away by saying Grandma Dollie had to have been drunk to say such a thing. Of course, Cody wasn't going to tell it. Had Grandma Dollie not come back into her room when she did, I would have been raped. Once things settled down, Grandma Dollie asked me if he had "touched" me anyplace, and I told her no. He had only been spooning me.

From that point on, Cody gave me the creeps. Every time he looked at me after that incident, I felt violated. Needless to say, I hated this man for years. It took years of prayer to the Lord to remove the loathing I held for him from my heart.

No one in our family liked him. If Momma Rosie and Poppa didn't like someone, that was really a strong statement. Yet, where Doretha was concerned, Cody was as enticing as the original forbidden fruit in the Garden of Eden. Somehow, she was psychologically dependent on this younger man who was only fourteen years older than me. I think the age differ-ence flattered her ego at some level.

Cody didn't become physically abusive to Doretha until after Wootsie shot him. He became hell-bent on dealing with Wootsie and I think that's what finally woke Doretha up. Wootsie never liked Cody from the start. He had attacked her sometime earlier and given her a black eye because Wootsie had warned Doretha about him.

One day Cody had Terry, his and Doretha's baby boy, in his arms, just tossing him up in the air with reckless abandon and catching him. The child was terrified and crying. Wootsie was standing in her room with her gun watching them with a bead on Cody. She said, "He could've dropped dat baby if he wanted, but I was gon' drop him dead right where he stood, had he done it." I wasn't far from Cody; I was terrified he might drop him as well. As soon as Cody put him down, Terry ran right to me crying his little head off. I think Cody resented the attention given to him because he was such a handsome little boy.

Cody must have seen Wootsie poised with her gun staring at him through the window while he was throwing the baby up in the air. That enraged him all the more. After he got enough liquor in him, he decided he was going to whip that old woman's ass again.

A year or so earlier, Cody beat Wootsie up but Doretha continued to date him. I remember seeing Wootsie with a swollen black eye, and she never forgot it. But Doretha would not listen to a negative thing about him. Cody found out that Wootsie had bad-mouthed him with Doretha and attacked her from behind at a house party. Wootsie never knew what hit her. Even though Cody had physically assaulted Wootsie, she didn't report it to the police. She didn't want to have them around the place where they might have become suspicious of her bootleg still. Doretha broke up with Cody for a short time after the incident, but in her typical poor judgment in such matters, went right back to him. Her view on relationships was, "If you can't be with the one you love, anyone else will do."

Eventually, the situation with Cody became so toxic that even Doretha couldn't handle it anymore. She put Cody out and forbade him to set foot on the property. He wasn't having it. Cody insisted that he was there to see his son, but I'm sure he had other motives.

He determined that it was Wootsie who had encouraged Doretha to get rid of him, and he told Wootsie he was going to whip her ass. Wootsie kept a .45 pistol and as I said earlier, was a crack shot. Cody came breaking up in the house in one of his tirades threatening Wootsie, who was in her room on her bed. Wootsie said, "Boy, you bed' not come in this room botherin' me." "Whose gon' stop me, *you*, bitch?" he responded. When Cody set foot in Wootsie's room, she rolled over on her stomach, took aim, and shot him in the left leg.

"Bitch, you don' shot me! You don' shot me!" He took another step in her direction and Wootsie put another bullet in the same hole. The bullets were backed up behind each other. The second shot broke his leg. Cody went down screaming like a little girl cursing Wootsie. I had to run out on the road and call an ambulance because our telephone wasn't working at the time. The ambulance took Cody off, still sobbing in pain. Wootsie whispered to him as they took him off, "I told you not to mess with me, you summa' bitch."

The police eventually came, but Doretha took the blame and said she had shot Cody. They took her in for questioning where she made a statement. Doretha claimed she shot Cody in self-defense. The police were aware Cody had been harassing her for some time but had not attempted to harm her apart from the occasional push or shove physically.

Just as a precaution, we took the German Luger Wootsie had used and hid it up in the woods. We were afraid the police would confiscate Poppa's gun, but they didn't even ask about it. Cody told the police that it was Wootsie who shot him, but Doretha swore she had done it. She said Cody had come to the Hollow unauthorized and barged into the house drunk. The ambulance attendants confirmed they had smelled whiskey on him. Doretha was more credible, and we backed up her claim that Cody had been harassing us.

In her official statement, Doretha said Cody had been on the property and in the house illegally and had something in his hands that she thought was a knife. When he raised his hand to strike her, she fell to the floor and shot him in the left leg. She persuaded the police that if she had intended to kill him, she could have simply aimed for a different part of his body. She had all of us as witnesses to back her up, if necessary. He didn't have a leg to stand on. The police brought Doretha back home after she gave her statement.

Fortunately for Wootsie, Doretha had taken out a peace warrant against Cody, so she had more justification for shooting him. Even after being shot, Cody did not give up coming to the Hollow uninvited until Pokechop came along . . . .

14

Pokechop

When Doretha was about seven, she was living with Uncle Ramey and Aunt Alice. She remembered a young man in his early twenties staggering to her uncle and aunt's store holding a coat to his stomach. As it turned out, someone had cut him across the stomach and his intestines were exposed, so the coat to his abdomen was to keep them from falling out. Uncle Ramey put this young man in his car and took him to the hospital to be sewn up. This was Doretha's earliest memory of William Estes, Jr., better known by most (and feared by some) as "Pokechop."

Pokechop was born in Maybeury, West Virginia, in 1912. His daddy, William Estes, Sr., had been a big-time bootlegger who lived between Maybeury and Bassett. Pokechop ran away from home when he was twelve. Word had come to his daddy that Pokechop had died, so he named a subsequent son

William Estes, Jr. So, Pokechop's daddy had two sons with the same name.

Pokechop had been a hellraiser even as a teenager. He became known for challenging authority and just being defiant. All these qualities, of course, drew Doretha to this dangerous, handsome older man like a fly to sugar. Pokechop had gone to war and survived it, been jailed a few times, and lived *la vida loca*.

He had initially come to Koehler Hollow to court Grandma Dollie. Yes, Pokechop's first romantic interest was in Doretha's mother. The two had known each other when they both worked for the Bassetts. Dollie cooked and Pokechop drove. But Dollie simply wasn't interested in him like that. In her strange logic, I think Doretha decided if she dated this older man she could rid herself of Cody, because everyone knew just how mean Pokechop was. When Doretha expressed her interest in him, he figured he would have a younger and, from his perspective, prettier woman. That's how they started dating. Grandma Dollie didn't seem to care about Doretha and Pokechop as a couple. She had finished with dating and shut down that part of her life.

I believe Doretha did the math to realize that she needed a husband to help her with her expenses, not to mention that she had a daughter about to go to college as well as younger kids. Pokechop had a disability check attached to him in addition to a steady job as a chauffeur. They dated a few years and married in 1971.

I was always a little afraid of Pokechop because he could be awful mean. Some said his shadow hid from him because he was so mean At least that was the joke at the time. But I admired him as well. Christine thought he was crude, but after a while I grew to love him dearly. Apart from George Washington Finney, Pokechop was the only other man I called "Poppa." He had gained my respect even before he and Doretha married.

Pokechop stood about six-foot-six with wide shoulders and had a John Wayne swagger.[1] He was a larger-than-life person and had a personality and presence to match. He was a proud, dark-skinned man with serious eyes.

Pokechop ran off Doretha's old boyfriend, Cody, which is when most of us began taking notice of him. Doretha and Cody had stopped seeing each other, but that monster was hell-bent on making our lives in the Hollow miserable. In fact, he made our lives hell most of the time that he and Doretha were together.

Cody would hide behind the house and terrorize Doretha. Once or twice, he roughed her up while she was going or coming from work. When she would have to leave in the morning to catch a ride to work, David had to walk with her to just keep that fool at bay. Once, David, my brother took Poppa's German Luger when he was walking Doretha. Sure enough, Cody showed up to harass Mother. He had parked his car

---

[1] John Wayne appeared to be drunk when he made most of his movies.

nearby and had slept in it. When that ass Cody appeared out of nowhere to threaten Doretha, David pulled out the Luger, fired off three shots in the air, and yelled at Cody, "You better get the hell out of here, or the next time I *will* be aimin' at yo' head." David was about sixteen at the time. Cody took off running so fast, he left dust as he fled. He was ultimately a coward when another man didn't allow himself to be bullied. But that evil man had the temerity to take out a warrant on David saying my brother tried to kill him. When the policeman came to investigate, the officer asked David if he had fired the gun, and David admitted he had done so. But he also explained that he never took aim at Cody and had only fired up in the air as a warning. He said he had been protecting his mother from Cody as she went to work. Fortunately, the police knew Cody had been harassing Doretha. The policeman said, "Since you told the truth about firin' the gun when most people would'a lied, I'll ignore it this time." He told David not to let anything like that happen again. And that was the end of the matter.

Some nights Cody would just come and bang on the side of the house or yank out the antenna wires so we couldn't watch television. Once, we just sat in our home terrorized. Even our yellow dog, Rennie, would hide under the house when he came along. All of that changed in 1968 when Pokechop came into our lives.

When he started dating Doretha, Pokechop already had an established reputation for being ornery. One day, Cody decided to come around the house and cause some trouble. Pokechop was inside the house and eyed him, but he kept quiet. Doretha went out on the porch to confront Cody for being on the property. Pokechop stepped out on the porch in front of her saying, "Get behind me, 'oman." He pulled out his .38 pistol and shouted in Cody's direction, "Shotgun! Shoot 'em 'for he run now . . . ," after the 1965 hit song by Jr. Walker and the All Stars. Pokechop was also a crack shot even when he was drunk. He took aim and put a bullet within inches of where Cody stood. That fool jumped off the ground about three feet, it seemed. Every time Pokechop shot at Cody's feet, he leapt up in the air. It looked like a scene from a cartoon to see Cody jumping up in the air after each shot. Pokechop got off about three or four shots before Cody took off running hard and fast. Those of us who witnessed this scene did so with wide-eyed amazement. It was kind of funny when I think back on it. It may have been the last time we ever saw that monster in the Hollow. I remember the shooting incident so well because it was July Fourth. *We* were celebrating because we had finally gotten rid of that wicked Cody.

Professionally, as I said, Pokechop was a chauffeur for the Bassett family. His driving skills made him a terror on the road if he chose to be. He drove a 1951 green Chevy pickup truck that he kept in pristine condition. You know how dogs like to chase moving cars? Well, Pokechop often slowed his truck to let a dog get near the driver's door. Then he would quickly open the door and knock the dog down, sending them tumbling on the road.

Another time some thuggish boys in Martinsville waited out on certain corners. As drivers slowed down to make right or left turns, they attempted to intimidate and rob people in their vehicles. They targeted elderly men and women. Seeing an older man driving by, one of these boys took Pokechop as an easy mark. The boy jumped up on the runner of Pokechop's truck, put a gun to him and said, "Give me yo' money, ol' man!" Steering the car with his left hand, Pokechop calmly grabbed his gun with his right hand, put it between this boy's eyes, "Boy, if you don't git yo' Black ass off my truck, I 'om kill you." The boy was so startled by how quickly Pokechop had put the gun up to his head, he dropped the pistol he had been holding, which turned out to be empty. He said that boy's eyes widened with fear to the size of golf balls. The scared boy could only get out, "I'm sorry, suh. I didn't mean no harm, suh. There was nuthin' in the gun." Pokechop then saw the boy peeing on himself which really agitated him. He stopped his truck and grabbed the boy by the collar, "I ought ta' shoot you for pissin' on my damn truck. Take yo' shirt off and dry my truck, boy." "Yes suh," the young man did as he was told. Pokechop then threw him on the ground with his urine-drenched pants and shirt.

Another time, when Doretha was in the truck with him, Pokechop was trying to pass a White woman in the car ahead of him. The woman was half-drunk and swerved all over the road. When she realized that Pokechop was trying to pass her, she sped up to prevent him from doing so. He simply pulled back behind her, which clued Doretha that he was up to something. Pokechop eventually caught up to the drunken woman at an intersection. All of a sudden, he accelerated and rammed her car in the back. He then pulled around her and kept driving. Doretha said the woman must have been startled, because when she got out of her car, she could see the woman had pissed all over herself. She called out some curse words at Pokechop, but he never paid it any mind. His favorite expression in such situations was "Wreck 'em!" As I said, he could be a mean man.

When I first met Pokechop, he didn't say much. I just knew he was a big, dark-skinned man that Doretha rode off with. I really took notice of him when he ran Cody off. *Then*, he became my hero and was okay with me after that.

Doretha had a job at a furniture factory in Bassett before I left for college. While she was at work and Pokechop was off duty, he and I would drive around to different junkyards and collect rubbish, which we resold. It was Pokechop who taught me how to use a penny to determine if a tire was still roadworthy. As long as there was enough tread to cover Lincoln's hair, the tire could still be used. We simply threw it in the back of his pickup and kept moving.

Pokechop became the quintessential daddy and became extremely protective of me. He and I also collected bottles off the side of the road in addition to our junkyard scavenging trips. Once we collected seventy dollars' worth of bottles. Doretha never appreciated me junkyard-hopping with Pokechop. As far as she was concerned, "What's a college gal doing huntin' round in junkyards? You' embarrassin' me." I could have stayed home and watched soap operas, or I could be out with Pokechop rummaging through junkyards for things to sell. The junkyard it was. When Pokechop got his monthly veterans check, he'd tell me, "We goin' to Shoney's today gal." He'd let me order whatever I wanted. I never asked him for anything that he didn't give me.

At Virginia Union, one semester I didn't have enough money for my $180 organic chemistry textbook. I had worked at a lab on campus and was going to be paid, but the delay meant I couldn't get my chemistry book until my paycheck came. I called Doretha and asked her for a $180 loan. One night when Pokechop came home drunk, she went into his wallet and stole the money and sent me a money order for the amount. Before the money order arrived, however, I got my paycheck and bought my book. I wrote Doretha a thank you note and sent the money order back to her. It never dawned on me to keep it. She said that was one of the most dull-witted things she had ever seen. "I stole that money from Pokechop. How in the hell am I gon' put it back?" As it turned out, however, Pokechop got the money back after all. He got caught drunk driving and his bail was set at $1,800. Ten percent of that was $180, so Doretha just signed that money order over to the court to pay the bail.

Pokechop had a very colorful past. He had been drafted into the U.S. Army in 1942 at age 30, just as things were going bad for the U.S. military. He served as World War II was raging in Europe. Of course, someone as cantankerous and defiant as Pokechop would never have enlisted. He had been dodging the draft for months before the military caught up with him. He simply kept catching the train between Virginia and West Virginia to escape the draft notice. The Army caught up with him when he was arrested for fighting. While he was serving his time, the outstanding draft notice caused him to be detained. He was taken right from the jail cell to basic training. I forgot where he was in boot camp, but it was somewhere in the South.

While he was in training, he had this White drill sergeant who routinely called his black troops "niggers." Wherever he was, the Black soldiers rioted to protest their conditions before they were sent overseas. On their first day of deployment to Germany, the same jackass drill sergeant told his Black troops, "Now don't ch'all shoot to kill, 'cause after all, these other fellas is still White." Once they neared confrontation with the Germans, the sergeant told his men to dig foxholes for themselves. He specifically ordered Pokechop to dig a foxhole for him. Pokechop enthusiastically said, "Yes, sergeant!" Soon afterwards, the Germans started shelling their position. The sergeant ordered his men into their foxholes. He ran around looking for his space but couldn't find it because Pokechop hadn't dug one for him. After the shelling stopped, the soldiers found the sergeant's helmet and one of his boots with his foot and ankle still inside. That's about all that was left of him. Pokechop never repented for not digging that foxhole. In fact, every time he told that story he laughed.

Because he was a trained machine gunner, Pokechop fought in several major European theaters throughout the war. In fact, he was a proper killing machine.

In Italy he received a head wound that troubled him for the rest of his life. He lost part of his skull and the military put a metal plate in his head. Had that been a White soldier, such an injury would have been his ticket back home. But the U.S. Army determined that it needed its seasoned machine gunners and sent Pokechop back into the field. In June 1944, he was part of the Normandy invasion in France.

Pokechop's 92nd Infantry was also known as the "Buffalo Division" during the war. The men in this unit proudly wore their distinctive olive-green-and-black Buffalo insignia patches on their uniforms. As they were crossing the Atlantic back to Norfolk, a White Southern colonel on board ordered the Black soldiers to remove their Buffalo patches and issued them a replacement patch no larger than a quarter. When a few of the Black officers protested the colonel's actions, he just said, "I can't have you niggers going back home with a case of the bighead thinkin' you somethin'. I want all them patches." Pokechop refused to take his off, so a lieutenant came along and ripped it off. The nearby soldiers had to restrain Pokechop from attacking the lieutenant. This guy then dismissively flipped him the quarter-sized replacement which hit the ground. The men were poised to stage a protest on the ship but were talked out of it by the Black enlisted officers who said their military careers would be hurt if they were somehow linked to any such action. The officers did report the colonel and cited his remarks, but that was about it. Every time Pokechop told that story, tears welled up in his eyes. He was a tough man, but even he had his limits.

Make no mistake though, Pokechop was tough. He once used a carpenter's nail in his mouth to kill some exposed nerves in one of his lower right molars. This tooth had been bothering him for weeks and he was too stubborn to go to a dentist. He heated up that nail until it was red hot. He put a rag in his mouth to cover the surrounding teeth, stuck the tip of that red-hot nail right into the cavity of that tooth, and bit down on it. Water rolled off his face like he had been in the shower. A few seconds later, he took a swig of liquor, swirled it around in his mouth, and spat it out along with a lot of blood. After all that, he went to bed. His jaw was a little swollen the next morning, but other than that, he was okay.

Although few people saw it, Pokechop had a soft side. When he first started dating Doretha, the toilet pit in the yard had filled up. He and another man dug a new toilet and built a new outhouse, which remains on the property. People who weren't afraid of Pokechop liked him. He had shrapnel all over in his body because of his war wounds and was in chronic pain. He drank, in many ways, to medicate himself. That head injury he received during the war caused him to have periodic excruciating headaches. It was esophageal cancer that ultimately caused Pokechop's death. Toward the end, he had a tracheal tube inserted in his throat and couldn't speak.

* * * * * * * * * * *

When I was about nineteen, we were living in Bassett. Doretha told me to pick up several items including a loaf of bread. I took her car and was on my way back home when I remembered I had gotten everything but the loaf of bread. I was driving on a two-lane highway. I'd already put my blinker on to turn left when I realized that I had forgotten the bread. I turned my blinker off and started to move forward. When I took off my blinker, this foolish man who had been following me too close decided to go around me on the right and I clipped his bright yellow El Camino. He was totally in the wrong because it was illegal for him to have passed me. I didn't hit him hard, but our cars made contact. Well, that little blond-haired White man got out of his car and started cursing me like I was a dog. He called me all kinds of bitches and stupid and this and that. I just stood there with tears streaming down my cheeks, because I had never been cursed by a grown man before. He was no taller than me, but I guess he thought being a man gave him an upper hand.

Somebody ran and told Pokechop I had been in an accident. This man was standing in front of me cursing away. The police finally showed up—an Uncle Tom Black policeman, Ben Smith. He didn't tell the man to shut up and stop cursing me. The White man continued to rant about how stupid I was for hitting his El Camino. Since the man was facing me, he didn't see Pokechop walk up behind him. The next thing you know,

Pokechop laid his big hand on this man's shoulder. When the boy turned around and looked up at Pokechop's six-foot-six frame, he was startled and backed down. In fact, I could see genuine fear in his eyes. Pokechop said, "You know boy, I can pay for yo' car, or I can pay for yo' ass, but you will not cuss my daughter—not one more time." That White man was staring into the eyes of death, because I knew Pokechop was about ready to gut-shoot him there on the spot. Ben Smith jumped between Pokechop and the White man and said, "We ain't gon' have this, Pokechop," who promptly responded, pointing at Smith, "I ought to bash you upside yo' head for lettin' this fool cuss her in the first place."

We set up an appointment to meet at the police station. Ben told Pokechop we had to pay to fix the White man's car. He was wrong, because the White man had made an illegal pass. We ended up having to pay $356. That amount is burned in my head. Pokechop put the money on the table, got up and walked out. Pokechop never said a word to me about the accident, but I have never forgotten what he said to that man.

* * * * * * * * * * *

Although Pokechop had a well-deserved reputation for being incredibly mean and surly, he could also be comical. He was as tough a man as I've ever known and had the biggest hands that I've ever seen on anybody. Pokechop was also as strong as an ox. He usually stayed about half "lit," but there was a reason for his reliance on alcohol. He was proud of his service in World War II, but the war haunted him the rest of his life. As I said earlier, his war wounds were so severe that typically a soldier in his position would have been sent back to the United States. But, like many African American soldiers who had special skills, Pokechop was simply patched up, and, when he was able to walk again, sent back into another battle theater.

He drank because he was in chronic pain. I guess the liquor helped to numb the physical and emotional injuries. Several African American fighting men came back to southwestern Virginian suffering from similar situations as a result of the horrors they had witnessed in the war. At that time there was no veteran's administration to help these men with post-traumatic stress disorder, although they had all served proudly. When veterans acted out after returning home, they were simply described as "shell shocked." It was a common expression of the period.

Pokechop often went hunting and would shoot three or four squirrels or rabbits. He'd walk into the house and drop those squirrels or rabbits on the kitchen floor. Doretha would be so mad she'd turn red in the face. He expected her to go skin and clean those animals. She did but would curse the whole time. Doretha hated cooking. Most of it had been done by Momma Rosie or Grandma Dollie. All things considered, however, Doretha and Pokechop made a good couple.

One morning around 10:00 AM, Pokechop came to me and said, "Gal, come take me up to Anderson's so I can get a littl' drink." We had a 1964 Dodge Dart with push-buttons. The road getting to Anderson's was full of gullies. It had been an old logging road. It was like driving under a tunnel with branches. When we got to Anderson's, Pokechop said, "Gal, you stay in the car. You don't want to be out with these fellas. Dey a no count bunch." He didn't need to tell me that, because I hadn't planned on getting out of the car anyway. It was bad enough being with Pokechop when he was half drunk. I certainly didn't want to be with them.

After he staggered over to the entrance of the bootleg joint, this fella said to Pokechop, "Who's that in the car?" He said, "That's my daughter. She's a college gal, so don't you go out there messin' wit' her." Well both of them went inside. Sure enough, that fella who Pokechop warned came staggering out the joint in the direction of our car. He was kind of light-skinned and had a little goatee. He looked kind of like the devil to me because he had red hair. The next thing I know, Pokechop had come back out of the liquor joint and pulled his pistol and shot at this fella's feet—pow, pow, pow! The man was almost at the car when he shot at his feet. When the bullets hit the gravel, some of it came in the window of the car where I was sitting, so I dove across the seat to keep from getting hit. The light-skinned man turned around and said, "Nigga, is you crazy?!" Pokechop hiccupped and said, "You damn right I am. But you take one more step towards dat car, and you will be dead." Need I say anything further?

* * * * * * * * * * *

When he wasn't wearing his chauffeur's uniform, Pokechop wore green khakis and a white flat-top hat. He also sported pork-chop sideburns that ran down his face. I believe that's where his nickname came from. Few people in this area knew of a "William Estes, Jr.," but if you asked who "Pokechop" was, they knew right away. As he aged, his white hair contrasted with his smooth, beautiful dark face, giving him an even more distinguished appearance.

One Saturday he and I were at the post office waiting for Doretha to get off work in Bassett. She only worked half days on the weekend. While waiting, we saw Delegate (and future Virginia Speaker of the House of Representatives), Albert Lee "A. L." Philpott walking down the street. Pokechop recognized him from his dealings with the Bassett family. I, of course, didn't know who he was. Pokechop said, "Gal, that's A. L. Philpott. He's in the government and works for the House of Delegates. When he gets up here, I'm gon' introduce you to him 'cause he's in Richmond and you can call him if somethin' happens to you up there."

As A. L. approached us, Pokechop reached up and pulled off his white cap and said, "Mister Philpott, how are you? I want to introduce you to my daugh . . ." Before he could get "daughter" out, Philpott said, "Boy, I ain't got no time for you right now," and kept walking. He wouldn't even stop for a second. Pokechop just stood there. He put his hat back on his head. The sweat popped off him and he grabbed his stomach and sat back on the ledge and clenched his jaw. That public snub hurt Pokechop to no end. The one thing he had to be proud of was a daughter doing well as a university student, and this politician wouldn't even let him finish his sentence. To make matters worse, he humiliated him by calling him "boy" in front of his daughter. I despised A. L. Philpott from that day forward regardless of the progress he made politically. I also never forgot that insult.

Twenty years later, in 1990, I ran on the Republican ticket against him. It was the best money I ever spent. I had taken over a Republican mass meeting by bringing twenty-two black people and got myself placed on the ticket. Yes, I had switched parties to run against A. L. Philpott. The Democratic ticket had already been set up, so I couldn't run against him on that side. Ward Armstrong had opposed him in the primary.

As the race progressed, I argued that A. L. Philpott had done little for Black people and he had kept industry that would have assisted us out of Henry County. It was for naught, however, because A. L. Philpott died during the campaign. He was replaced on the ticket by Ward Armstrong. At least A. L. heard the accusations I made against him and his record, even though he was on his deathbed. Revenge is a dish best served cold. Watch what you say to people. Anyone can rise up against you in the long run. Just for your information, Ward Armstrong defeated me in the race.

* * * * * * * * * * *

After several difficult months in the hospital, Pokechop died on November 3, 1981 at the VA Medical Center in Salem, Virginia. In addition to developing throat cancer, he had other debilitating illnesses. Some of those had dated back to the time of his WWII service. Although he passed away more than forty years ago, I remember as if it were yesterday.

It was a Tuesday. The day before, Doretha and I had battled a snowstorm to get to the medical center. Pokechop was barely coherent, but I believe he sensed our presence in his room. I kept speaking to him and massaging his arm. I only stopped long enough to wipe away tears streaming down my face. Even though he and Doretha had their ups and downs, they were devoted to each other. She just sat in a chair in his hospital room as if in suspended animation and didn't say much. Doretha and I left at the end of visiting hours, and he died during the night.

When we made it back the following day, we were told that Pokechop had passed away at about 4:00 AM. The attending physician knew we were coming back later that day, so he elected not to call us that early in the morning. I don't remember Doretha reacting too much, because I think she was relieved he was no longer in pain. The military arranged for his remains to be sent to West Virginia for burial.

Christine, Doretha, and I drove up to Maybeury for Pokechop's funeral. Although Grandma Dollie was still with us, she elected not to go. One of his sisters, Buster, was there along with his younger brother of the same name, William Estes, Jr. I hadn't been to that many funerals prior to Pokechop's. Looking at Pokechop so still in that casket seemed to be the very antithesis of the person that I came to know and love. Initially, tears were running down my face, but then I chuckled when I suddenly remembered the story of him purposefully bumping into that woman's car when he was with Doretha, and it caused her to pee all over herself. I just imagined that woman jumping out of that car cursing him. My tears turned to smiles as I thought about the many other stories he told me over the years.

After the funeral I noticed the custom of other drivers clearing the way when a funeral procession is driving by. I also saw men, both Black and White, stand still and remove their hats while the procession passed—a Southern custom of respect for the deceased. As the funeral procession approached the cemetery, it was as if the entire town had collectively said, "We're sorry your daddy is gone." Even though I was thirty when Pokechop passed, as he was being buried, I remembered the feeling of security he had given me years earlier when he entered my life. He was as much of a protector as any father could be. His death was tough.

Pokechop left behind his Maine coon cat named "Big Foot." He was a mixture of a lynx and a domestic cat, which meant he had a huge head with a majestic mane, almost like a lion. His body was equally impressive. Although he was gentle in the house, your average dog stayed clear of this cat, because he could whip a dog's ass without breaking a sweat. That cat could be as mean as Pokechop. He was so heavy you could hear him walking around the house. While Pokechop was in the hospital, Big Foot mostly sat on his shoes waiting for him to return. He didn't move much from that spot even though he had been away for months in the hospital. That cat must have sensed that Pokechop had died because he acted normal before that. It was like the cat was protecting his master's shoes for him until he returned. He'd walk off to eat and do his business but came back to those shoes. About two weeks after Pokechop's death, Big Foot left the house and never came back. He surely grieved the death of his master and just left.

Years after Pokechop was gone, his reputation for being mean and tough continued. I was playing golf about six years ago and this White man came along and asked if I wanted to join him. Following Southern custom, he asked, "Who are your folks?" I told him I was a Finney from Fieldale, but my stepfather was William Estes, Jr. He looked at me in surprise and said,

> "Lord, gal. Yo' daddy was Pokechop?! He cost me some money. I lost $500 bettin' against him in a bare knuckle boxin' match. The guy fightin' him was bigger and younger and I thought this guy was a sure thing to win. Yo' daddy put up his dukes and was just rockin' back and forth

and he moved forward on this other fighter. Although yo' daddy took a few good licks, he eventually put that other fighter down good."

That was a story I had never heard before, but I knew every single word this man had said was true. I chuckled to myself and thought, "Pokechop must have been smiling in heaven or wherever he was saying, 'You see, gal? I told you I was somethin'."

15

Grandma Dollie, Doretha (and me)

I saved this narrative for the end. It's hard for me to open up about one of the biggest mistakes of my life. It involved my grandmother, my mother, and me.

I lived with a negative dynamic between Grandma Dollie and Doretha for most of my life. In short, it was horrible. When I married Honey, Doretha was still living in Bassett. Pokechop had died and Grandma Dollie was over seventy. Truth be told, Doretha was showing her age too. Her legs seemed to hurt all the time. After Wootsie died in 1985, I told Doretha, "Why are you living in Bassett when you can live with Grandmother at the Hollow? I've moved out." I never should have done that. Doretha moved in with her mother and was like hell on wheels. I regret to this day that I did it.

Grandma Dollie was asthmatic—Doretha would drench herself in White Diamond perfume and give Dollie asthma attacks on her way to church. She spoke to Dollie like a dog. She'd slam doors and slam pots around the house and was just plain horrible to her mother. Grandmother would tell me how horrible she was. I attempted to get her to understand things from Doretha's point of view, which was frankly a Herculean task.

I thought that somehow by getting those two together, they could reconcile—that somehow, they would bury the hatchet and tell each other they loved one another. But that didn't happen. I was totally wrong for putting those two in the same living space. The relationship was too damaged to be repaired, and neither of them could say they were sorry. At one point, Grandma Dollie asked me if she could move in with me. I didn't say no, but I also didn't say yes. I was convinced by forcing those two to live together, they would at least learn to tolerate each other.

When Doretha was living with Grandma Dollie, I picked my grandmother up every Saturday to take her shopping and to hear how things were going with Doretha. I bought her whatever she wanted and sat in the car, where she told me how horribly Doretha had treated her. She had even cursed Grandma Dollie. Somehow, I couldn't quite bring myself to believe Doretha was capable of acting in such a manner. I had never seen that side of her. I concluded that Grandma Dollie surely had to be exaggerating. But I came to see that Doretha was capable of incredible rage. I also believed she was psychologically impaired. It was like living with two people. One was a sweet person whose brain elevator didn't go all the way to the top floor. I never saw the malicious part that she sometimes showed. After all, she had little reason to show it to her children. But I knew it was there.

Back in the 1950s, in addition to her regular work at Jobbers Pants Factory, Doretha took on a part-time job in the evenings and weekends at the Henry Hotel working as a maid. The White manager paid her every Friday. She had worked the job for several weeks and was expecting to get paid one Friday, but the manager said he would pay her the following day. Doretha went to see the manager for her money the following day, but he refused to see her and ignored her calls. There were several people in the lobby of the hotel when she cornered him. Doretha drew her knife and put it up to the manager's throat. "I need to buy groceries to feed my chaps. You give me my money. Don't make me cut ch'you." The stunned guests in the lobby saw this small Black woman threatening the tall White man. Several laughed at the manager, but Doretha was as serious as a heart attack. The manager paid her the money, and Doretha ended her service at the hotel.

Things didn't go south with me and Doretha until she found out that Grandma Dollie and Wootsie had deeded Koehler Hollow to me solely. We had a different relationship after that. You might wonder how that happened? Well, Doretha was entirely to blame for the entire situation. By the time I finished at Virginia Union, my younger brother Terry had become a textbook definition of a hoodlum. He had been kicked out of school for taking a knife to the principal's car tires. He had become a truant student and was eventually sent to Leary Educational School in Winchester, Virginia, which is a facility for youths with serious emotional disturbances. Terry was declared "psychologically impaired with criminal tendencies."

Well, the very first bill I inherited after completing my education was the $176 monthly invoice from Leary, which Doretha handed over to me. Terry stayed in Leary until he was about fifteen but was kicked out for walking up behind a female instructor and choking her by wrapping a towel around her neck.

He then went back to Bassett, where Doretha was living with Pokechop at the time. Pokechop would never have put up with any of Terry's foolishness and would have whipped his ass right from the beginning. He probably needed it. I don't doubt Pokechop's discipline would have straightened him out. But Doretha sent Terry to Koehler Hollow, where Wootsie, Grandma Dollie, and I were living. He was nearing sixteen, prone to be rebellious, and feeling his oats.

Terry begged me to cosign for him to buy a car. I told him I would help him if he got a job. He agreed. I helped him to find a janitor's job at South East Container, so we bought him a used yellow Mustang. Terry worked the job for two weeks before quitting, leaving me with his car payment. Inside of a month, Terry totaled the car. I said to myself, "Thank you, Lord! With the insurance settlement, the car will be paid off." Terry then said I "needed" to cosign for him to get another car. Of course, I told him no.

"Not only did you wreck the car you had, but you have shown me that you are irresponsible and won't keep a job. Our agreement was for you to get a job. What did you do? You quit after two weeks."

Terry nearly went berserk. He accused me and everyone else of never caring about him, which caused his life to be so messed up. He was nearly foaming at the mouth. He had borrowed an old broken-down rifle from a neighbor. Everybody knew it was broken, but he pointed it at me, Wootsie, and Grandma Dollie. I gathered Dollie and Wootsie, both of whom were in their sixties at the time and took them out of Koehler Hollow. I then called the police. I explained to them that Terry might need a psych evaluation because of his tantrum. The police took him to a facility in Danville. Somehow, Terry managed to escape from that facility.

The police called to warn me that he had broken out and that I should be on the lookout, because as he was being arrested and transported, Terry had made clear he intended to kill me. When Terry inevitably arrived at Koehler, he kicked open the door in a rage. David was there to calm him down. The police recaptured him, and he served a short while, but was eventually released after Doretha pleaded his case and persuaded me to not press charges against him. I decided to leave Koehler and go to Bassett, but that still left Terry and his volatile temperament with Wootsie and Grandma Dollie.

A day or so after Terry's flare-up, Wootsie and Grandma Dollie went to a lawyer in Martinsville and deeded Koehler Hollow over to me. They were so disturbed that Doretha had once again disregarded her responsibilities and sent her psychologically damaged son with criminal tendencies to two women in their sixties to handle. They had had enough.

I need to make clear that Koehler Hollow was not handed over to me arbitrarily as a gift or as a vengeful act against Doretha. When I returned from college, the homestead was in a deplorable state. There was no plumbing in the house, no furnace, and the roof was leaking. Doretha knew the family was living in these conditions but didn't have the means to do anything about it. Wootsie and Grandmother gave it to me because I made all those repairs and more. Wootsie and Dollie also thought Doretha would not be a suitable steward of Koehler Hollow and the surrounding land that had been left to them by Poppa and Momma Rosie.

They also knew that had the homestead been put into Doretha's hands, she would attempt to leave it to all of her children even though she knew some were not as responsible as others. When I told Doretha this after she found out Grandma Dollie and Wootsie had deeded Koehler Hollow to me, she flew into a rage.

"Koehler Hollow is *my* birthright. You stole it. You' a thief."

"No Mother. I didn't steal anything. Grandma Dollie and Wootsie willed it to me. I didn't ask them to do it."

"No. You' a thief."

"No, you did this to yourself."

"Well, give it back to me, then."

"No, I will not. Grandma Dollie and Wootsie said I am only holding this land in trust for the next generation. If I were to give Koehler Hollow to you, Terry would come back and say, 'Give me my portion,' and then it would have to be sold. Our family's legacy would then be lost. Grandma told me to give it to *one* of the nephews or nieces, because I don't have children."

None of what I said dissuaded any of Doretha's rage. On her deathbed, she called me a thief. We are now five generations after enslavement and that land remains in our family. The property itself is only worth $33,000, which isn't that much. But to hold land that has been in our family for five generations in trust is everything. To be able to say this is land that a formerly enslaved woman bought, and we continue to hold it several generations later, is beyond a price tag.

Doretha couldn't appreciate any of that. Because she had been so angry at her mother, she interpreted leaving Koehler Hollow to me as Dollie's final slight against her. Similarly Grandma Dollie believed Doretha sending her criminally insane son to Koehler, where she knew he could easily turn violent, was a calculated action on her part.

This toxic dynamic was the consequence of bad parenting. I learned that you should love your children even when they are old, because they will look at you. You will either be the benchmark or the nemesis in their lives. Don't get me wrong, I loved my mother and I have missed her every day since she died. I have also missed Grandma Dollie. She was in many ways the heart and soul of this family.

But Doretha felt Grandma Dollie did not love her. That, no doubt, contributed to several of the reckless decisions she made throughout her life. Doretha treated Wootsie better than she treated her own mother. She also loved Momma Rosie. Doretha recalled that when she got her first job working at Jobbers Pants Company, one of her proudest moments was giving Momma Rosie a crisp five-dollar bill. In total fairness, Doretha put electricity into Koehler Hollow and bought our first refrigerator and washing machine. She really honored Momma Rosie and Poppa. Her principal nemesis was her mother, Dollie.

* * * * * * * * * * *

A few years before her death, Grandma Dollie was diagnosed with a stomach aneurysm. At the end of July 1996, it ruptured and we had to take her to the hospital. At eighty-five years old, the doctors warned us that she was not likely to survive a surgical procedure to remove it and we should prepare for her to die. I remember the doctor saying she would likely pass on within a day or so. Doretha glibly declared, "Well, I'm going home." So everyone left Grandma Dollie except me.

Before she lost consciousness, she asked again if she could come and live with me. I fought back tears as I said, "Of course you can, darling." She smiled faintly and I thought she went to sleep. It turned out she had slipped into a coma. I was told by the hospital staff that I should also leave. I told them,

"No, I'm not leaving her."

A nurse said, "Well, you can't stay here in the intensive care section."

"The hell I can't. This is my grandmother. She didn't come into this world by herself and she's not going to leave by herself," I asserted. So, they left me alone in the room with Grandma Dollie lying peacefully in her bed attached to a respirator.

Around 3:00 AM, that room got very cold. The top of my head felt like it was freezing. People can say there is no such thing, but I believe the death angel came into that room. I asked myself, "How can this room be so cold?" That's when I heard the high-pitched squeal indicating a flatline from the machine monitoring her. Grandma Dollie quietly slipped away.

After the nurses came in and detached the monitors and removed the machine from the room, I just sat there and stared at how peaceful she looked. I had a brief flashback to when I used to crawl up in her bed after I'd follow her down to her house when she drank too much. As I looked at her so peacefully, she had entered an eternal sleep. I was strangely comforted by that thought. I didn't cry. I just sat and guarded her lifeless body. Even then, I felt she still needed me.

I called Doretha at about 5:00 AM. I could manage no more than a whisper because if I had attempted to speak at my normal voice level, I would have broken down. When she answered the telephone, I managed in a soft voice to say,

"Grandma Dollie is gone." Doretha suddenly became excited and said, "What!? Aren't they doin' CPR? What are they doin' to bring her back!?" I quietly told her, with my voice trembling, "She had a Do Not Resuscitate order in place. She's gone." As if I hadn't said a single word, Doretha continued on, "Well, I wan 'em to bring Dollie back!" I kept quiet. Despite the surge of anger that came over me, I forced myself not to slam the phone down on her. I just quietly placed the handle back into the receiver. It was a classic "a day late, and a dollar short" mentality. She had treated this woman horribly in life and now wanted her back.

Years later, when Doretha was living with me, I understood things better. In fact, I experienced every single negative behavior of hers that Grandma Dollie had described to me, multiplied by at least two. Doretha's hell-raising and belligerence was right in my face with an added twist.

Prior to her developing dementia, Doretha and I had some wonderful times. We had several grand adventures every weekend. It was great fun. But then, Jesse Ben Hodge, my birth father and Doretha's estranged first husband, came back to Martinsville to die, and that poisoned our already volatile relationship. Of the fifteen or so years that Doretha lived with me, the last three years were torturous. An already-fractured relationship went further downhill.

In 2005, Jesse Ben Hodge was in a hospice facility in Cleveland with cancer. The place contacted me and asked if I would honor his wish to be brought back to Henry County to die.

He had listed me as his daughter. Bill was already in a nursing home at that point, and it was costing me $5,000 a month to keep him there. So, I flew Jesse Ben back here and placed him in my recreation room in a hospital bed. I was still working full-time, so I asked Doretha to assist me with some minor tasks for her former husband. She had not forgiven him for his actions from years earlier. In his time, he had beaten women. I didn't realize how much it pissed Doretha off to help him in any way. He was with me for about three weeks before he was transferred to a hospice facility in Martinsville.

Jesse Ben passed away shortly afterward. Doretha thought she was due money for those weeks she looked after him. All she did was give him some soup or other small things. She didn't bathe him or help him on or off the commode, because the hospice people came to tend to those kinds of needs.

Jesse Ben had left his descendants a small piece of money, and Doretha felt she was entitled to some of it. I explained to her she was not one of his descendants, but she wasn't hearing any of that. I had to bury Jesse Ben on a wing and a prayer. The little money in that policy, which amounted to about $2,000, didn't cover his funeral expenses.

Somehow, Doretha felt she had been cheated and there was no talking her out of it. What she was churning around in her brain just didn't match reality. Christine and I spoke to a woman at the Social Service office that manages survivor's benefits. That agency only contributed a few hundred dollars to defray funeral costs. The case manager was prepared to give us a cardboard casket, but I thought that was going too far. We had to get $300 from one family member and $400 from another. The funeral home sold us a wooden cremation casket, which we happily took. Jesse Ben's brothers and sisters supplied the balance. We buried him for less than $4,000. We cut corners even further by having Christine preach the funeral. Aside from Doretha and his remaining brothers and sisters, we were the only ones present at the service.

Doretha had an "I been done wrong" feeling about not being compensated for assisting Jesse Ben, but once she had something in her head like that, that was it.

The Jesse Ben scenario had been my most recent negative encounter with Doretha, but the seeds of the conflict were already sown. The real brawl had begun seven years earlier when Grandma Dollie had deeded Koehler Hollow to me alone. Doretha never got beyond the fact that I was the sole owner of it all. As her dementia worsened, she called me a thief and a liar. I told her for the umpteenth time,

> "Mother, Grandma Dollie told you to your face that you would never be able to differentiate among your children and that Terry was a criminal. She said that you would attempt to leave the property to all of your children and it would have been sold. Grandma Dollie always said, 'If a slave could buy this land, how dare a free person lose it.'"

When she deeded the land to me, Grandma Dollie and Wootsie made me promise I would give Koehler Hollow to one of my nieces or nephews—not two, only one. Christine's daughter will inherit Koehler Hollow when I pass on. It will be her job to keep this property in our family. I am no more than a custodian of this land—its temporary owner. The transfer to her has already been signed and executed.

Well, Doretha wasn't having any of that. She continued to say, "You' a thief. Koehler Hollow is *my* birthright. I'm gonna sell all the trees off the land."

"No, Mother, you will not. I don't want to, but I will stop you, if necessary," I said quietly, but firmly.

"Well since I still live here, I will control Koehler Hollow and do what I want with it." I knew that threat was no more than blowing smoke, so I left the argument there.

So, Doretha rented a room in Koehler Hollow to some White thug who used it as a gambling joint on Saturday nights. Before Doretha moved in with me, she and Terry had lived there. Terry also moved his girlfriend in with him. That meant Doretha, Terry, and his girlfriend were living there. And this White fella was using it to gamble on the weekend. It was an affront to Poppa and Momma Rosie that their homestead would be used in such a way.

To add insult to injury, Terry would beat this woman on occasion, because she was bisexual. She liked Terry, but she also dated women. She'd be all right with Terry for a few weeks and then she'd leave him to hook up with a woman.

Terry would inevitably find out and they would end up in a fight. The reason Doretha ended up moving in with me is because Terry beat this woman one night and Doretha intervened. Terry cursed Doretha and she was about ready to shoot him. To diffuse things, I simply moved Doretha to my house.

Although I was living with Bill in his family house at the time, I could not become the owner after his death because he had structured a survivorship instrument that meant the house would automatically be owned by his son after my death. I decided I needed a house that I owned. I had just finished my MBA and hired an architect to design a log cabin on the site of Koehler Hollow. It was going to be a ranch-style, with Doretha at one end of the house and Honey and I at the other. In the middle there would be an open loft area. After the architect submitted the design draft, I left for a twenty-one day trip to Europe.

When I came back from that trip, Doretha was in an uproar, "I'm not gonna live in Koehler anymore. I've been up there for seventy-one years. I don't want you to build there. I wanna live in a community." I shook my head, "Are you serious?" I should have known Doretha was pulling a con.

She knew Terry and I would not get along and I was not likely to let him live in the new house I had proposed to build. Terry had also begun dope peddling and Doretha knew I would have him arrested before I tolerated any of that. I have come to believe that while I was in Europe, Doretha told Terry about my plans to build a new house on that site and he persuaded or cajoled her into blocking them.

The joke was on Doretha in the end. Within weeks of her tirade about wanting to "live in a community," Terry attempted to kill his girlfriend's lover. She had left Terry for this woman, which put him in a murderous rage. Right before he went off to kill this woman, Terry called me and said, "I'm a kill that bitch for stealin' my woman!" "Terry, who made you God!?" I told him.

> "You knew this woman swung both ways. There are plenty of short, black women who like men. Get yourself one of them! You need to leave that woman alone. You have no right to kill her lover."

Terry calmed down after that conversation, but it didn't take him a month before he had stalked the woman who had taken his girlfriend. He stole one of Grandma Dollie's .22 pistols and shot that woman in the face. Only by the grace of God did the bullet lodge behind her nose and not kill her. Terry was arrested and charged with attempted murder. Doretha wanted me to put Koehler Hollow up for collateral to get him a good lawyer instead of relying on a public defender. Of course, I rejected the very thought of it.

When the case got to trial, his former girlfriend's lover identified Terry as her assailant. Terry's former girlfriend also testified against him and corroborated his violent nature. The prosecutor paraded Terry's past criminal deeds to persuade the court that he was, in fact, a serial offender who had now graduated to attempted murder. According to the prosecuting attorney, he would have been successful in killing the woman had that bullet not stopped where it did.

The defense attorney called Doretha to the stand, and she told the court that when Terry had been young, he had pneumonia and had stopped breathing for a short while. That episode, she explained, caused his maladaptive behavior. But not even a mother's tears could stop a guilty verdict. Doretha cried inconsolably as Terry was convicted of attempted murder and battery. He served twenty years in jail and was released in 2018.

After Doretha came to live with Honey and me, I thought that would be the end of the issue of Koehler Hollow's ownership, but she still made the occasional remark about it. "David wants a piece of Koehler," she'd say.

"No, Mother, that's not how Grandma Dollie wanted it."

"Well, it's his birthright too," she'd say more insistently.

"It wasn't given to him. It was given to me," I'd say abruptly and end the conversation.

Towards the end of her life, I was nervous about even going to Koehler Hollow, because I was genuinely afraid that if Doretha even suspected I had been in that house she'd have one of her temper tantrums and give herself a stroke. Even at my house, she'd have such extreme fits of anger that I would take my dog and lock myself in my room to avoid her. She had dementia by then, which undoubtedly exacerbated her condition. Sometimes she would walk behind me as if she was holding a gun in her hand and pulling the trigger. "Pow! I could just shoot you." Just to avoid things, I took all the bullets out of her gun, or "pistolero" as she called it. If I had taken her gun, I knew she would have a fit.

Like her mother Grandma Dollie, Doretha also developed an aneurysm. Hers, however, was in her head. The day it ruptured, Christine had come to my house and told Doretha, "Let's walk around the driveway." I asked them not to, because the physical strain might be too much for Doretha's system. She said in her most defiant voice, "I'll walk it, or die." After she and Christine walked, Doretha came back in the house and went up to her room. She was there for less than two hours when the aneurysm ruptured just as I had feared. My surrogate son, J'Vontea, was living with us at the time. He took Doretha her food because she wouldn't take it from me. I believe she thought I had done something to it. She took one bite of food and slumped over in her room. J'Vontea came running down-stairs saying, "Something's wrong with Grandma Doretha. She just collapsed!"

We took her to the hospital for emergency surgery. They would have to shave off her hair to go into her head. Christine and I determined she would never have approved of such a thing, and we resolved to let her go.

On the day of Doretha's funeral everyone gathered at my house. The women in the family agreed to wear black and white. That church was full, but it was also very hot. I'm surprised no one passed out. Melinda honored her grandmother's request and played a saxophone solo at her funeral. I thought how much she would have enjoyed Melinda's performance at her homegoing celebration.

Doretha's death in 2015 was traumatic all the same. It's not easy to admit, but I had developed a codependent relationship with her. Because she lived with me, it became my responsibility to bury her. Things were arranged well. Doretha was, without question, a complicated woman. But she loved her grandchildren, and she was especially proud of her granddaughter Melinda.

Aside from Terry, who was still incarcerated, all her children and grandchildren attended the service. We laid her to rest next to Grandma Dollie and Wootsie. Perhaps that was a mistake, given her complicated relationship with her mother. What's done is done now.

In one of her more lucid moments late in her life, Doretha asked me to take care of her boys, especially Terry, because she knew he was the most vulnerable of her children. Proverbs 13:22 says that a good man leaves an inheritance for his children's children. Amy Finney, I honor you. George Washington Finney, Poppa, I honor you. Dollie Finney, I honor you. Your house and the land surrounding it still stands where it was built one hundred years ago. Doretha, your son Terry now lives in Koehler Hollow rent-free. I've fixed it up for him and I'll do all that I can for as long as I can to help him. That's my promise to you.

16

The Kinsman Redeemer

*F*or years, my sister Christine has referred to me as our family's kinsman redeemer. It's a biblical concept in which the senior male in a family is designated to act on behalf of his relatives who may need to be defended. He helps them to avoid trouble or gets them out of some difficulty, including financial trouble. The kinsman redeemer could also be a family spokesperson or a representative. It can be the relative who restores or protects the rights of disadvantaged family members or those in need. I believe such a role was thrust on me after I completed my undergraduate degree at Virginia Union University in the mid-1970s. Immediately after finishing school, I paid back taxes on my family's homestead before the land was lost. I saw it as my responsibility to bring this family into the twentieth century by installing indoor plumbing, extending the size of the house, putting on a new roof, clearing off some of the land to make it available to farm, and other necessary renovations. I have been responsible for this family in ways that many of them aren't aware of. I expect this book, for good or for bad, will correct that murky picture.

And so I have come to the end of this exercise that I began more than ten years ago. This work, as Christopher Brooks can attest, has taken many turns. It could have had a very different ending were Doretha still with us. But honestly, her death, which I have come to deal with over the last several years, gave me the opportunity to reflect on the impact she had on me, this family, and Koehler Hollow. As I told you, parts of this story are painful, but once all is said and done, we are a family that has survived as we as a people have survived.

In my role as president of the Martinsville NAACP, I have seen many instances of injustice in Henry County and throughout this region. Sometimes, I get overwhelmed in my thoughts of some of the battles I have felt compelled to fight down here. Oftentimes, I have felt like I had to stand alone without support from the very people who I am advocating for. As I am approaching my mid-seventies, I don't know how long I will be doing this job. But I'm waiting for a successor to take over this mantle. I'm sure they're out there. I've frankly been discouraged more than once. Like many African Americans in this part of the state know well, standing up to certain humiliations has become a way of life. Many don't have the will or knowledge to resist and simply acquiesce.

While I am still able to put my thoughts on paper, it occurred to me that I should give an account of our family and those who influenced us growing up in this region of the country. After all, when most people think about Appalachian families, they think about Whites. Now they will have an inkling about the African American experience dating back to Great-Great-Grandma Amy. The story of African Americans in Appalachia represents a long and extensive experience. The *Tales of Koehler Hollow* represents only a kernel of that experience. If we take into account the year of Grandma Amy's birth in 1850, and her subsequent enslavement on where Koehler Hollow stands, our family has been on that land for close to 175 years.

That brings me to my final point about our family legacy and it came from Grandma Amy. She told Poppa that our people from Africa had come from what is now modern-day Nigeria and that we were Igbo. Poppa pronounced it as "Eye-boe," as his mother had. I went to college with that information and told some Igbo students from Nigeria whom I met at Virginia Union about it. Poppa taught us an Igbo word that means spoonbread made of honey-powdered grain, but I have long since forgotten its pronunciation. Doretha said Poppa once prepared the dish for her, but also said it wasn't very good.

On Thanksgiving morning 2016, several family members assembled at the long-abandoned Mountain Top Cemetery in Fieldale to correct a fifty-two-year-old mistake. It should have been taken care of more than a generation earlier by members of this very family. At long last, we dedicated grave markers for

Poppa and Momma Rosie. He has been in the ground since 1964 and she since 1968. Neither had headstones at their respective interment sites. We started off the brief ceremony with a song and Christine preached a brief sermon marking the significance of the occasion. In her comments, she spoke about Grandma Amy, Poppa, and Momma Rosie, saying, ". . . were it not for them, there would be no us. So, to them, we need to be thankful." I also said a few words taking us back to our founding matriarch.

> "Amy Finney was born enslaved and died a landowner. She left us the land that is still in our hands today. She was a woman who could not read or write but had a cure for childbed fever. She was a businesswoman who plowed with two mules and never once backed down. Her son, George Finney, a reverend, a preacher who lived a Godly life before man. He walked right as a man of morals and ethics and always gave an 'honest day's work for an honest day's pay.' That's what Poppa always said, and I have lived by that example.
>
> George Finney set a standard of what manhood is and should be. And Rosa Waller, his wife, set the standard of what kind, Christian, loving women looks like. Momma Rosie never raised her voice. She was the blueprint for motherhood in this family.

We come here today to honor Poppa and Momma and let them know that even though they have rested here since 1964 and 1968, respectively, without a headstone, they lay here no longer unrecognized. We also want to let Momma and Poppa know we are thankful for who they were—poor, Black, and discriminated against. Still, they had integrity and gumption. And they did not walk through the world with heads bowed and spirits broken. They walked with purpose. So, we leave here saying 'Thank you, ancestors, and thank you, God for giving these people to us.' We have recognized them and taken this time to say, 'George Finney, we remember you.'

When I look at you young men here today, I remind myself that you are the seeds of George Washington Finney. Remember who you are. I don't care how bad it gets, George Finney didn't break. He didn't steal. He didn't do ugly things. He stood like a man. This is your DNA. You need to claim it and live in it . . . ."

Our final family correction was completed in February 2017 when we placed a headstone at the grave of our sister, Loretta. She had been interred at Mountain Top Cemetery unrecognized even longer than Poppa and Momma Rosie. There had always been a disquiet in my soul about not having seen to this. Now that Loretta's final resting place has been duly marked, I feel my soul is rested. It will now be up to my niece to take up the mantle when I am no longer able to. I have hopefully done my part and provided the necessary background to sustain the Koehler Hollow legacy for future generations.

Acknowledgments

*A*t long last Naomi and I get to thank so many who have participated in the realization of *Tales of Koehler Hollow*. This project was conceived more than a decade ago and has been a transformative experience for Naomi and me. Her commitment and tenacity to this project has been unmatched in my experience as a writer. When she began telling me these family stories, it took a little time before my writing senses began to tingle. When they did, it was full steam ahead. Naomi and I are pleased with the results. Important to these narratives is Naomi's younger sister and best friend, Reverend Amy Christine Hodge. Christine's recall, especially her reflections on her relationship with her and Naomi's great-grandmother, Momma Rosie, was critical in portraying the importance of this family matriarch.

As with my other works, Naomi and I need to acknowledge those who did not live to see this book in print, yet were pivotal to the telling of this story. Among them are Naomi's late husband and life partner, William B. Muse, Jr. He was a symbol of African American achievement, excellence, and determination. He was also one of the most decent men she has ever known. We also want to recognize Doretha Finney Estes, whose sometimes difficult and sometimes amusing experiences were critical to the life and legacy of Koehler Hollow. Naomi's Aunt Lizzie Stockton, while initially cautious speaking around a stranger, eventually reached a comfort level to identify certain geographical locations referred to in this work. Naomi's late mentor, Dr. Valley Wyndell Hylton, was able to provide us with context for several of the narratives contained within these pages, while also stressing the importance of education throughout his life. Dr. Dana O. Baldwin, a physician, developer, visionary, and community leader, was a beacon of pride throughout his ninety-seven years within the Martinsville area. He dutifully filled out Naomi's preadmission medical report as she entered Virginia Union University. During her lifetime, Naomi's late sister-in-law, the renowned Frankie Muse Freeman, was able to give details about her family and the challenges and triumphs they faced growing up in southwest Virginia. Sadly, Miss Alberta Wilson recently passed away in March 2024 at 101 years old. As one of the oldest living residents in the Martinsville African American community, she lived through many of the developments told in this book.

I am obliged to acknowledge many colleagues and offices at Virginia Commonwealth University, including the College of the Humanities and Sciences Dean's office and the office of the provost, especially Fotis Sotiropoulos, who charged the faculty to increase scholarly output. I hope this work will contribute to that mission. I should also acknowledge Amy Rector and my other colleagues in anthropology, from whom I have enjoyed support for many years.

My editors and commentators on this manuscript while it was in various stages of development deserve to be thanked, including Drs. John "Jay" Whaley, Emily Esola, Gerald C. Howard, and my late brother-in-law, Thomas J. Brown. I also want to thank my neighbor, Denise Bethel, Dr. Noel T. Boaz, and Andrew Chess, who was a high school student at the time this work began. Although I lost contact with him, I highly valued his input.

Naomi also wants to thank her cousins, Jackie Stockton Kordalewski and Patsy Riley-Smith, and friends Pauline Rorer and Carlton Stockton. Naomi wishes to acknowledge Beth Macy whose book, *Factory Man*, inspired her to pursue *Tales of Koehler Hollow*. We are also grateful to our editors Don Rosso and Amy Rath at Unsung Voices Books for bringing this overdue work to fruition.

I want to thank Charles Hackett, Jr., Sheryl Feuerstein, and Brenda and Eric Kahari (deceased) for listening to me through the various drafts of *Koehler Hollow*. Finally, I gratefully thank my brothers and sisters including Lowry M. Brooks, Joyce

Brooks Brown, Bernetia Brooks, Carroll Brooks, and Cheryle Brooks Johnson. Close to them would be my children David and Rahab, and my granddaughter, Eliana Amanda Brooks. Naomi and I want to again thank you all.

Christopher A. Brooks
Virginia Commonwealth University

Naomi Hodge-Muse has served as the president of the Martinsville chapter of the NAACP and Voter's League, and was appointed by two Virginia governors to the New College Institute Board of Directors. Hodge-Muse continues a family tradition of community activism and leadership in Virginia, which has included detailed historical research. She is a proud graduate of Virginia Union University.

Christopher A. Brooks is a professor of anthropology at Virginia Commonwealth University. He has produced numerous award-winning publications focusing on the African continental and diasporan experience. Brooks, an internationally recognized biographer, has authored a series of books exploring the HIV pandemic in Africa and America.

About Unsung Voices Books

Unsung Voices Books publishes books to better know other people the world over. Our publishing program centers around perspectives from writers from marginalized and underrepresented groups and ways of life and stories that enrich our understanding of the places that make up our world.